BODIES.

BETWEEN SPACE AND DESIGN

BODIES.

BETWEEN SPACE AND DESIGN

CRISTINA BIANCHETTI

jovis

PREAMBLE

This book was written before the spread of the coronavirus pandemic in February–April 2020, and it was written in a territory—northern Italy—that was severely affected by it. The pandemic caused the body to re-emerge in all its fragility. It repositioned the body in physical space, in social space, and in the space of control and the limitation of freedoms. First of all, the pandemic repositioned the body as sick, diffident, fearful, and reclusive. Secondly, it repositioned the vulnerability of the body, revealing its differential, fractured, and decomposed character. And, finally, it repositioned the mass of dead bodies: a terrible echo of Elias Canetti's words resounding in the many images accompanying the chronicle of this recent past.

The pandemic was a terrible natural experiment imposed on the relationships between bodies, spaces, and the project. The pandemic asked the project to rethink the density of space as a function of a body requiring protection—a body which, in order to protect itself and other bodies, deprives itself of perhaps the most fundamental faculty: that of touch. Touching other bodies, touching space, hitting it, skimming it, leaving your own imprint; dwelling in the materiality of the body. Reducing the ability to touch is an act of incorporeity in the sense discussed in the following pages: it is to detach the body from ourselves, to become a foreign part of it, to exorcise it.

The pandemic forced the project to think of a future in which density is reduced while safeguarding the interaction between bodies. However: "to preserve itself, the body needs a great many other bodies"—both human and non-human. This is the great crime perpetrated by the pandemic: it is the loosening of the ties of our subjectivities embodied in mistrust, safeguarding, and care.

Lesa, May 2020

AROUND THE BODY. INTRODUCTION

We are not a calligraphic
sign on a white surface,
an ornament.
We are a body that twists
into something with density,
and friction.
Moresco, 2009[1]

For all those involved with the city and territory, space refers to the body. This is first and foremost due to an enduring organic analogy that has been very important in the humanist tradition of western culture. The organic analogy has exploited the body to establish a morphology. It has done this by projecting it on the city, representing its ideal perfection, and finding words, proportions, and relationships in the body. It has pursued the body's authority in order to narrate the city, represent it, design it, make it the seat of the social and political body, and impose it on the world. The organic analogy has been powerful in the past and remains so. Anthony Vidler writes about its revival as part of a new appeal for organic metaphors in architecture, even if the body is now radically different: a body in pieces, fragmented, if not deliberately torn apart and mutilated,[2] indicating an explicit departure from classical humanism.

The organic analogy was powerful and still is. Nevertheless, my first argument is not inspired by this continuous re-emergence of the organic analogy and its vigour. Nor is it inspired by the impetuous re-emergence of the body in our daily lives, driven by canons of health, strength, and beauty: the new sanctuary where contemporary man consummates his alienation. Not a vehicle, but an obstacle to being in the world, patiently remodelled by physical exercises, diets, and the entire repertoire of rituality so very reminiscent of the spiritual exercises of sacrifice and mortification. They place the body in another dimension.

For all those involved with the city and territory, space refers to the body because we act, experience, and live in the encumbrance of our bodies.[3] Bodies are not "calligraphic signs": they are cumbersome and opaque; they have weight, occupy space, leave stamps, measure distances proportional to their gestures, gazes, and voices, and allow themselves to be crossed by them. They enjoy a carnal relationship with the world, which leads to an experienced, individualised dimension of space. The materiality deposited in names, signs, and practices conceals what counts as a body[4] in its relationship with space, which is unlike a "white surface". It is space crossed by impulses, desires, and renunciations; existential space that is neither geometrical nor anthropological. Awareness of one's own body coincides with knowledge of being in a place: it is the body's hold on the world. In space, "bodies wriggle free": they are always engaged in something practical. They are bodies that act and suffer. In space they meet other bodies with which they collide, ally themselves, and come into conflict. Phenomenology considers having a body to mean uniting with a defined environment, merging with certain designs, and continuously committing to them: "We must therefore avoid saying that our body is in space, or in time. It inhabits space and time".[5] Likewise, Sartre's existentialism claims that "this *being-there* is precisely the body".[6] We are united, merged, and involved with space. Even in Foucault's structuralism we unexpectedly find something very similar: "my body ... it is the absolute place, the little fragment of space where I am, literally, embodied".[7] In this small book, after having studied the mad, medicalised, surveilled, and punished body, Foucault writes about the relationship between the ego and the body, starting with the incredible coincidence that "it will always be there. Where I am": the ambiguous source of all experiences, but also of all utopias.[8] The discourse about the body is a discourse about the fact that we are engaged in the world: touched by, invested in, and enlightened by the world, as bodies in spaces.

"My body is the little fragment of space where I am, literally, embodied." Space belongs to the body. We live and act in space through our bodies.[9] We incorporate the directions, obstacles, resistances, and openings of space. We do not move forward according to the modernist epic of conquest, frontier, and hegemony. We do not remodel everything from scratch. Our being is active and passive: we act and we suffer. It is always a relationship of co-presence and reciprocal implication: the impact of collisions with other bodies and the world. We receive stimuli and react to them, we hear words and answer them, we elaborate the messages we receive. This means we are constantly exposed—but, at the same time, it is a sign of the body's consistency, substance, and power of action. Of its frailty. Through the body we are involved in intense processes of connection and interdependence: we meet other bodies with which we collide, ally ourselves, and come into conflict. We are exposed to others, to eyes that spy on us, surprise us, and covertly look at us.[10] We are exposed to encounters, we are transported towards others, we are capable of influencing and of being influenced. We are exposed to the system of norms, rules, and prohibitions that redefine our desires and our parental, sexual, and productive relationships. Or, speaking more generally: our life conditions. Feminist literature has focused extensively on the way in which normative matrices become the premises for models of a stable body.[11] In any case, the body cannot be reduced to a sign: it cannot be alluded to, implied, or suspended in the measurements or silhouettes establishing its contours. Relationships with space are built through physical experience: action, perception, and the senses. The body is "*the zero point of the world*".[12] Space opens up to us through our body; through its position, faculties, strengths, and frailties. And it also opens up to us through our fears, dreams, projects, and desires. Things are arranged according to the meaning they assume for the body. Space is luminous, dark, streaked, smooth, disquieting, dangerous, immense, or cramped because that is how the body experiences it. Sight, touch, and smell are the doors through which the world enters our bodies. What we are and where we are are what counts, as is time, because the body has memory of it: "My body .... its memory, the composite memory of its ribs, knees, and shoulder-blades offered it a whole series of rooms in which it had at one time or another slept; while the unseen walls kept changing, adapting themselves to the shape of each successive room that it remembered, whirling madly through the darkness. And even before my brain, lingering in consideration of when things had happened and of what they had looked like, had collected sufficient impressions to enable it to identify the room, it, my body, recalled ...".[13] This is one of the most famous literary images of the twentieth century.

Bodies Between Space and Design: About This Book

The body is a "*canale di transito*" (transit channel)[14] between space and design: the go-between with which design manipulates space. This is the critical position proposed in this book. Design always alludes to a space either filled with bodies, or void of bodies. Of bodies in their material finiteness. Of relationships: of bodies that either ignore or search for one another. Of antagonisms. Of alliances. It is not the perfection of organic analogy (challenged only by the imperfection of Frankenstein's monster) but the material solidity of the body that makes itself visible, breathes, moves, stays still, speaks, or remains in silence. It manifests its own intimacy: little, insubstantial habits. It exposes itself. The body has knowledge of its relationships with other bodies and with space: it is an "extremely delicate device"[15] in the relationship between space and design.

This is the point of observation from which I examine several twentieth-century architects, urban planners, and landscape designers representative of a primarily European tradition. They are individuals who developed important ideas about the city and architecture, alluding either directly or indirectly to the theme of the body: Richard Neutra, Clair and Michel Corajoud, Alexander Klein, John Habracken, Paola Viganò, Bernardo Secchi, and John Turner. Extensive literature has been dedicated to these authors, often over a long period of time. I certainly do not presume to present a critical outline. But I will use fragments of their ideas and projects to illustrate my theory of how important the body is in urbanism. Each of these authors will help pinpoint the relationship between spaces and bodies using different viewpoints and sensitivities. Recalling their approaches also means recalling the approaches of many other authors, designers, and critics. Without presuming to reassume anything, I will try to propose a possible order in the next few pages, well-aware that my greatest difficulty is relinquishing the numerous positions of other urban planners on this theme.

I have uncovered some of the ways in which bodies and space are related within the endless intricate ties linking the urban project of a city and its architecture to a body that can either be healthy, sick, or dead; a body that needs to be removed, hidden, or treated, as it has been in hygienism, therapeutic architecture, or popular walkscape practices. Or urban project may be linked to a hedonist body, a pleasure-body, a body that is open to the world. A body that invents itself, recomposes itself, and replicates itself until it becomes a body lost in an oceanic sentiment; a sentiment that is almost religious, as Sigmund Freud stated with regret in his book *Civilization and Its Discontents*.[16] Or a body that is guarded, scrutinised, and measured in eighteenth-century judiciary anthropometry, as well as in the measurements and gestures in space of the great season of the avant-garde. A body that looks and searches for gazes, as in El Lissitzky's self-portrait.[17] Or, on the contrary, a body afraid to be seen; a body that perceives the gaze from noises, as in Jean Paul Sartre's walk in the woods.[18] Or again, the body in the crucible of psychoanalysis that transforms relationships with the clients, in restless psychoanalytical sessions in the United States in the fifties, or in Lacanian circuits between *extimité-intimité* where what is important is "that which is foreign to me … is at the heart of me".[19] The removed body of Habraken's structuralism: a non-existent body that leaves its stamp, that acts and suffers. And in addition to these, the body in a relentless accumulation of different versions: Gordon Matta-Clark's body in pieces; the body without organs; the post-organic body, expressing a not-so-discreet fascination for technology. The freed, emancipated body, the body that claims its rights, the body visible, the body's expression of its desire for affirmation. The body in the gravitation of mass; the famous photograph of Terragni's Casa del Fascio in Como during the assembly of the Fascist Party in 1936 is its most disconcerting architectural representation.[20] The impetuous body of the *Multitude*, the orderly body of the community. The alliance between bodies in the space of feminist thought. The visible body of the public space of politics, in the sense intended by Arendt. The list is destined to remain open-ended.

I will focus on several of these figures and examine explicit and implicit ways in which urban projects and designers use the body; its opaqueness is ambivalent. I wish to highlight the strong points, not the linearities. Urban planners discussed the aporias of narrative a long time ago[21] and much water has flowed under the bridge since, triggering enormous diffidence towards the discursive as well as spatial figure of continuity (I use Bernardo Secchi's words differently).[22] The season of structuralism broke down narratives and, through its most famous and opposed author, Roland Barthes, reaffirmed the power of the fragment.[23] Even before then, Thomas Kuhn had demonstrated how even in the reassuring field of the hard sciences, linearity was fractured and disjointed,[24] while Stephen Jay Gould discussed the discrete and unrepeatable nature of balance.[25] In other words, the abandonment of linear reconstructions is inherent in urbanism, at least for my generation. I don't know whether this is good or bad, but it's difficult to avoid.

My procedure involves accumulation. I've tried to do my best with the data provided by texts and designs. I've observed the ways in which designers and their projects modify space by alluding either directly or indirectly to the body: a full body that sees, feels, moves, and changes, one that is with other bodies that acknowledge one another, that have reciprocal relationships of indifference, exchange, collaboration, and competition. My interpretation is based on the framework I outlined at the beginning of this introduction. I assume that the body is open to the world (and that this state of being open to the world defines "what a body can do" in terms of knowledge and action); that knowledge is founded on perception (that things are arranged around the body and that space is experienced in the encumbrance of bodies); and that internal-intimate reality cannot be reduced to mere intimacy. I think it is clear to which ideas these three propositions refer; propositions which I have humbly assumed neither sequentially nor to reformulate any theories, but instead to find data to support my reasoning.

This approach allowed me to discard the references to the body adopted in many dualisms: the religious and spiritual dichotomies that pit the body against the soul and spirit (present at least from the time of Homer's epic with *psyche*—the breath that exits a wound or mouth of the dying leaving only the cadaver of the body). Christian tradition is based on the ontological schism between the body and a spiritual entity; on the one hand, it reproposes the separation of the immortal and mortal part of man, and on the other revives the body as the channel of union with the community.[26] The most important schism, however, is not religious. It involves Descartes. His entire philosophy can be considered a reflection on the body.[27] Here, the body is always considered from an external viewpoint; always from a mental point of view. For Descartes the mind does not coincide with the body— but to recognise itself it must distance itself from the body and become independent, as the mind and body are made of different matter.[28] And it is this schism that leaves an impression in language: separating *Körper* and *Leib*. On the one hand, there is the body reduced to an object: the physical or material body. An ensemble of organs; the body-object, the body-representation. The body-I-have. The body that occupies a space, that can be represented in detail, can be measured, can be described in its form and functioning. The body that builds facts and practices through the dissected cadavers in Vesalius' canvases, in Rembrandt's public anatomy lessons. On the other hand is the subjective side of the body; the experiences I have had, I alone, of my body—of the *body-that-I-am. Leib* is the body and the way we experience it in life. Phenomenology would say: *I do not have a body; I am a body.* In biology and history, feminist thinking would claim the overcoming

of every dualism: the body is not a place of appropriation: it is not the owner of a self, conscience, or soul. The body is not mine. I am the body.[29]
These dichotomies have built the history of Western thinking. They recur constantly. They cannot be put aside once and for all. However, my reasoning is not based on these dichotomies.

What Is Urbanism?

In the past dynamic season—the last few decades of the twentieth century—urbanism was interpreted based on the concept of place; place as *context* (Vittorio Gregotti), *palimpsest* (André Corboz), *statute of places* (Alberto Magnaghi), *ground* (Bernardo Secchi), *uncultivated* (Lucius Burckhardt), and *site* (Sebastien Marot). Dwelling, producing, and exchanging have profound roots in places—and so do urban projects. This statement is almost superfluous. It is something that clearly and manifestly characterises the European tradition.[30] Who can forget Siza's white sheet, used to hide and at the same time reveal every little deviation, depression, and protrusion of the ground?[31] European urbanism is founded on the relationship with a solid place, consisting not simply of material, geographic, and morphological signs but of values, norms, and rights. *Context, palimpsest, ground, site,* and *uncultivated* are concepts that transmit the weighty, visible, steady character of things. For Marot, "the site is like a volume"; a mix of multiple stratifications "between the lithosphere and the atmosphere".[32]

Furthermore, European urbanism did something else: it considered space through the body, as I shall try to demonstrate in the pages that follow. It questioned what passes between the body and space: trust, rights, battles, contrasts, tensions, memories, conflicts, exchanges, pleasure, enjoyment, longing, turmoil, empathy, power, technical organisation, and actions. By doing so it implicitly or explicitly interpreted the site as a *place of the body* and, as such, as multiple, mobile, vulnerable, volatile, tenacious, powerful, and fragile—as all bodies are. Not as an impression, a "calligraphic stroke", a persistence or permanence of actions over time—but as a *space of the body* measured against the great questions placed before us by the present moment: health, sickness, ageing, environmental changes, the plurality of practices, and the political nature of space. These are the topics design has to tackle through the body. It is this aspect of my reasoning that I wish to highlight. It is this other kind of urban planning, nestling within the first, that I wish to discuss.

I trust that the observations in this book will prompt other observations—be they in accord or disagreement—and demonstrate that European urbanism is more complex and profound than the many simplifications that exist in this field. I have, for some time now, been convinced that the rift that occurred between the 1980s and the first decade of the twenty-first century has called into question the practices and know-how of urbanism—and that this has triggered the need to rethink the latitude and strength of design.[33] Reasoning *about the body* should be considered a step in this direction.

Notes

1   Antonio Moresco, *La visione.*
     Conversazioni con Carla Benedetti,
     Milano: Libri Scheiwiller, 2009: 44
2   Anthony Vidler, *The Architectural*
     Uncanny. Essays in the Modern Unhomely,
     London: MIT Press, 1992; Antoine
     Picon, *La matérialité de l'architecture,*
     Marseille: Parenthèses, 2018
3   This idea was developed by Gabriele
     Pasqui during his lesson "The horse,
     Deleuze and Spinoza", (21 November
     2018), *Urban Planning Course,* Prof.
     Cristina Bianchetti, Master's Degree
     Course: Architecture City Construction,
     Politecnico di Torino, Academic Year
     2018–2019
4   Judith Butler, *Bodies That Matter: On*
     the Discursive Limits of "Sex", New York:
     Routledge, 1993
5   Maurice Merleau-Ponty, *Phenomenology*
     of Perception, London: Routledge, 2002
     (first ed. 1945): 161 ff.: "In so far as
     I have a body through which I act in
     the world, space and time are not, for
     me, a collection of adjacent points nor
     are they a limitless number of relations
     synthesised by my consciousness, and
     into which it draws my body. I am not in
     space and time, nor do I conceive space
     and time; I belong to them, my body
     combines with them and includes them.
     The scope of this inclusion is the measure
     of that of my existence; but in any case it
     can never be all-embracing". p. 162
6   Jean-Paul Sartre, in *Being and*
     Nothingness. A Phenomenological Essay on
     Ontology, New York: Washington Square
     Press, 1992: 461 proposes a relational
     perspective on this issue: being there is
     also "the shock of the encounter with the
     Other", "the revelation in emptiness of
     the existence of my body outside as an
     in-itself for the Other".
7   Michel Foucault, *The Utopian Body,* radio
     lecture delivered in 1966. Published in
     Sensorium, Cambridge: MIT Press, 2006:
     229–234, cit.: 229 "My body … because
     it is around it that things are arranged.
     It is in relation to it – and in relation to
     it as if in relation to a sovereign – that
     there is a below, an above, a right, a left, a
     forward and a backward, a near and a far.
     The body is the zero point of the world.
     There, where paths and spaces come to
     meet …" p. 233
8   Ivi: 229
9   "The body is our general medium
     for having a world", Merleau-Ponty,
     Phenomenology of Perception, cit.: 169
10   Topic extensively studied by
     Sartre in *Being and Nothingness. A*
     Phenomenological. Essay on Ontology, cit.
     and present in other books I have used
     in my research: the aforementioned book
     by Foucault and the essay by Jean-Luc
     Nancy in *Corpus,* New York: Fordham
     University Press, 2008
11   For example, Butler, *Bodies That Matter:*
     On the Discursive Limits of "Sex", cit.
12   See note 7.
13   Marcel Proust, *In Search of Lost Time,*
     Edited and annotated by William C.
     Carter. New Haven: Yale University
     Press, 2013, in *"Swann's Way",* n. pag.

14 Term used by Roberto Esposito, *Le persone e le cose*, Torino: Einaudi, 2014: IX

15 Ivi: IX

16 Sigmund Freud, *Civilisation and its Discontents*, London: Norton, 2005 (first ed. 1930)

17 El Lissitzky, *Self-portrait (The Constructor)*, Los Angeles: The Getty Research Institute, 1924

18 Sartre, *Being and Nothingness. A Phenomenological Essay on Ontology*, cit.: 347. "What does *being seen* mean for me?"

19 Jacques Lacan, *The Seminar, Book VII. The Ethics of Psychoanalysis, 1959–1960*, Jacques-Alain Miller (edited by), New York: Norton & Co., 1992

20 A photograph revealing its unsustainability turned into a photomontage in the opening pages of Peter Eisenman, *Giuseppe Terragni Trasformazioni. Scomposizioni. Critiche*, Macerata: Quodlibet, 2004: 9

21 Bernardo Secchi, *Il racconto urbanistico*, Torino: Einaudi, 1984

22 Bernardo Secchi, *Prima lezione di urbanistica*, Bari: Laterza, 2000

23 Roland Barthes, *A Lover's Discourse: Fragments*, New York: Hill & Wang, 2010

24 Thomas Kuhn, *The Structure of Scientific Revolutions*, Chicago: University of Chicago Press, 1996

25 Stephen J. Gould, *The Flamingo's Smile. Reflections in Natural History*, New York: Norton & Company, 1985

26 See the topic "*Hoc est enim corpus meum*" return in the first pages of *Corpus*: "We're obsessed with showing a *this*, and with showing (ourselves) that *this* this, here, *is* the thing we can't see or touch, either here or anywhere else – and that *this* is that, not just in any way, but *as its body*. The body of *that* (God, or the absolute, if you prefer) – and the fact that *"that" has a body*, or that "that" is a body (and so we might think that "that" *is the* body, absolutely): that's our obsession". We have to insist: "I'm telling you truly that *hoc est enim*, and that I'm the one saying this: who else would be so sure of my presence in flesh and blood? And so this certainty will be yours, along with this body that you'll have incorporated".

"But the anxiety doesn't stop there: what's this this, who is the body? This, the one I show you, but every "this"? All the uncertainty of a "this," of "thises"? *All that*? Sensory certitude, as soon as it is touched, turns into chaos, a storm where all senses run wild" Nancy, *Corpus*, cit.: 3 and 5

27 Esposito, *Le persone e le cose*, cit.: 80

28 The shift between the dual Cartesian substance and the two modes of a single substance is the path indicated by Spinoza. Baruch Spinoza, *Ethics*, London: Penguin Books, 1951: Part III Postulate I, Part II, Prop. XIII

29 Merleau-Ponty *Phenomenology of Perception*, cit. Nancy, *Corpus*, cit.

30 Towards the end of the nineties, Vittorio Gregotti in particular insisted that there was a European tradition: see Vittorio Gregotti, *Identità e crisi dell'architettura europea*, Torino: Einaudi, 1999; the book came out at the same time as the last issue of *Casabella* under his direction: no. 630–631, (1996) "Internazionalismo critico". Even the magazine *Rassegna. Questioni di architettura e di progetto*, also directed by Gregotti between 1979 and 1999 (Publisher CPIA Bologna), focused on similar topics in several monographic issues; for example, issue no. 51, *Architettura nelle colonie italiane in Africa* (1992) and issue no. 65, *Architettura e avanguardia in Polonia 1918–1939,* (1996)

31 Alvaro Siza, "Professione poetica", *Quaderni di Lotus*, Milano: Electa, (1996)

32 Marot adds that "*Le site [est] comme un volume*", Sébastien Marot, "De l'art de la mémoire a l'art de l'espérer", in Panos Mantziaras and Paola Viganò (eds.) *Urbanisme de l'espoir*, Genève: Mētis Presses, 2018: 189–216, cit.: 189

33 Cristina Bianchetti, *Il Novecento è davvero finito. Considerazioni sull'urbanistica*, Roma: Donzelli, 2011

THE SICK BODY

The idea of purity and impurity must be yielded.
Neutra, 1954[1]

California in the Fifties

In the first half of the fifties, many fears were rife in the United States. The signs were everywhere: in the repeated sightings of unidentified flying objects; in the global nuclear nightmare detonated by the mushroom cloud over Hiroshima; in the ghosts of environmental pollution; in the belief that the environment itself could be a real threat to man's physical and mental wellbeing. Variously described and manifest phobias and neuroses were everywhere. The golden age of American noirs that starts with *The Maltese Falcon* is a good reflection of the atmosphere of fear and infatuation with psychoanalysis and expressionist oneirism.[2] The metropolis and the desert were contrasting geographical and metaphorical spaces onto which concerns, phobias, obsessions, and experimentations could be projected. Both represent scenarios of a civilised world[3] in which survival is crucial. In his book *Survival Through Design*,[4] Richard Neutra provides an excellent illustration of the anxieties of those years; of the belief that "man may perish by his own explosive and insidious inventions".[5] Long before it became popular, *environmental design* was a pressing issue for many people.[6] All this seems very recent, but in fact we're talking about the distant fifties.

The Austrian architect Richard Neutra is one of the protagonists of modernism in architecture: he was Otto Wagner's pupil, Adolf Loos's collaborator, and Erich Mendelsohn's assistant in Berlin until 1923, after which he moved to the United States where he met Frank Lloyd Wright and Rudolf Schindler.[7] We know a lot about Neutra's relationship with Freud; he was a friend of Freud's son (who also became an architect) and often met with Freud, eventually beginning to use psychoanalysis as a tool for his own introspection and in his profession.[8] He himself provided glimpses of all this,[9] including in his long review of Edward Hall's strange, rambling, and forward-looking book *The Hidden Dimension*, a psycho-anthropological study

on the meaning of being in space—or rather, on the ways in which we perceive space through our senses.[10]

The environment in which Neutra worked in the United States after the
war was permeated by the attention to psychoanalysis adopted by a rich,
educated clientele concerned about themselves, their bodies, and their nightmares. To paraphrase one of Deleuze's expressions, "psychoanalysis worked
in the open air", rather than enclosed between the walls of a studio or hos-
pital, where the psychoanalyst assumes "the status of a merchant in feudal
society which, according to Marx, functions in the free pores of society; not
only in private studios, but in schools, institutions, sectorial groups"[11]—and,
we would add, within professions. In this interplay between psychoanalysis
and architecture, Neutra sought a new design that used emotions, fears, and
traumas as materials; a design that acknowledged the unconscious and followed its desires. I feel it is more productive to interpret his architecture in
this (not unusual)[12] direction than in the two preferred by critics. The first
of these is well-presented by Bruno Zevi in his essay on Neutra; it is based
on the differences between designing architecture in Europe and the United
States and is concisely expressed by the statement "emigrating is difficult
for everyone ... either one remains basically European ... or one is assimilat-
ed".[13] The second is based on ideas of luxury and glamour and is summarised
in the few scathing words that Allison and Peter Smithson dedicate to the
architect—or, rather, to the photographs of his houses, which they thought
were characterised by "a kind of de-materialised glamour, almost that of soap
and toilet paper advertisements".[14] The first of these two critiques involves
traditions and assimilations, the second the circuits of communication and
the market. These paths are not separate, but divergent.

Neutra is a fascinating, magnetic figure. Manfred Sack considered him a
"Modernist, Missionary, Lover of Nature, Philanthropist".[15] Neutra himself
would have preferred to be defined as an "architectural therapist". He was
certainly considered charismatic by his students, who were photographed
crowding around him and looking at him ecstatically.[16] He paid great attention to his public image: all his photographs were precisely staged. For
example, the one published in the *Times* on 15 August 1949 shows Neutra
sitting with a client in a meticulously arranged interior.[17] The photograph
reproduces a Hitchcock-style setting—or, if you prefer, a confessional scene.
Is not psychoanalysis also the result of the proliferation and institutionalisa-
tion of the confessional procedures of our civilisation?[18] These photographs

reveal Neutra's penchant to model his role as an architect on a therapy session: he wanted to satisfy his client's psychological needs, to imagine and build an architecture in which physical consistency had a direct emotional effect. The construction of an emotionally intimate bond became a necessary condition of interpreting space as a therapist.

Neutra tackled a key topic in psychoanalytical theory: the repression and sublimation of the libido. He considered Freudian sublimation to be a transformation of energy, or in his words: "transformation of repressed energy into a symptom".[19] The problem facing architects was that of tackling the changes in energy that define the relationship between man and the environment.[20] Neutra wrote to Freud that the latter's idea of a "sublimation of sex energy into something else was very analogous to the idea of energy transformations".[21] Architecture, being in itself a body, is no longer a system of proportions, or a machine for living in, but a flow of powerful energies transformed in space. It is yet again, if you like, an organicist analogy, albeit one with a difference: what is being projected in space is not the harmony of the proportions and ratios of the body, but the impurities and adulterations of life. So much for the search for purity in modernist space.

Limiting the Unconscious or Producing the Unconscious?

The ability to interpret the client's stories and produce spaces capable of interacting with the unconscious required a well-oiled therapeutic machine, suitably represented in the photographs of Neutra with his clients. This is the design concept for his extraordinary houses: brash, polished, luminous modernist houses, combined with stretches of water reflecting the transparency of the Californian sky; swimming pools, open-air lounges, huge glass walls that frame the very beautiful, estranging landscape when looking out from inside, and the study and bedrooms when viewed from the outside. Houses with "spider legs" (long pilasters and steel beams anchored to the ground); uterine spaces mediated by the external environment.[22] It was an attempt to connect a desirous economy with technical, acrobatic expertise.

The therapeutic triangle between the architect, client, and house is tested in each design, and it is clearly unique every time.[23] The most famous of these cases (or stories) involves the Lovell House; even for the lukewarm Zevi, its structural boldness was exceeded only by Frank Lloyd Wright's *Falling-water*.[24] The owner of the Lovell House used to write the column *Care of the Body* in the Sunday edition of the *Los Angeles Times*, in which he talked about his ideas on health and the virtues of healthy nutrition, sunbathing, nudism, and sporting activities. The culture of the body was already present in Europe in the thirties and was relaunched by the upper class in California after the war.[25] However, the story of Clarence Perkins is the most useful one for discussing the viewpoint proposed here; it is also the best story for demonstrating how empathy transforms the architect-client-house triangle.[26] The *Perkins House* (1954) is "one of Neutra's most romantic interiors,"[27] in which the simple layout is hidden through the varied use of solid and transparent interior walls. Big glass corners create niches in a living room that opens completely onto the landscape. The continuity of the layout is complicated by visible beams, light systems, and wavy patterns on the ceiling. It was a successful exercise involving the typical dialectics of Neutra's architectural works: between intimacy and the landscape, hidden places and disclosed views, vegetal essences or rocks and glimpses of the desert.

Neutra was unbearably self-absorbed and usually considered arrogant; he didn't mind telling everyone that his clients were enamoured of his ability to empathise; that it was an uncalculated, spontaneous, and innate gift. "This is what happens. There is a tragic touch to the heroism, I assume".[28] And so it was for the *Perkins House*: the young woman was an ideal figure with which to measure the architect-client relationship that became a passionate shared bond. The object of that bond was not the woman's body but the house; the object of their joint empathic and psychic projections. A house that was no longer, and not only, a house. For Clarence Perkins, it was a space free from the memory of a despotic mother and the pain of the loss of a father.[29] A house in which to project desires and failures. "A house of therapy."[30] Neutra also believed in the therapeutic effect of the house, which he visited "whenever he felt low"; in those rarefied spaces he felt himself to be an architect, analyst, confidant, and patient. The house was "not so much their dream house as the house where they would work through their dreams, their mood enhancer and the instrument of their self-analyses".[31]

What is evident here is the reversal of the concept of an analytical position of benevolent neutrality, typical of an orthodox psychoanalytical technique, in which the therapist creates the schema on which the patient can project and critically relive his or her anxieties. The position of the architect is that of an empathic, deformed, never neutral, detached, impersonal mirror. Empathy is a shift from the technical terrain of design to the body; a shift that bestows grace on the architecture. "This is what happens." In the opening of this paragraph I cite Deleuze: "It is not a question of reducing the unconscious; it is much more a question for us of producing it".[32] The question is: under what circumstances, and with the support of what events, can the unconscious be produced politically, socially, and historically? The *Perkins House*, designed sixty-five years ago in Pasadena, California, shows just how much the design of space can fuel the unconscious.

Neutra's work is an interesting crossroads at which to explore the area of affect intensity that insinuates itself into the cold, rational space of modernism. The architectures are clean and perfect—so much so that they appear impossible to reach. They triggered the Smithsons' rather presumptuous irony. In that cold, rational, perfect, clean space, design relocates disturbed bodies, unsolved traumas, and infantile desires.

A Question of Survival

Survival Through Design was published in 1954. More than ever before, the issues that threaten us today are a question of survival.[33] Atomic nightmares have been replaced by climatic, environmental, and social nightmares: pollution, diseases, ageing, habitat alterations, the extinction of traditions, languages, and cultures, and so on. Faced with the dark clouds gathering overhead, we urgently need to wake up. Or rather, we need to reposition; something untiringly repeated by current literature about our Anthropocene age.[34] As in the past, design now takes centre stage as the repairer and replenisher, capable of "allying with other protagonists of the universe"[35] from bacteria to silkworms. Design is hailed as a plural practice capable of facilitating new ways of producing mobility and economic growth. Capable of redesigning relationships between fields of knowledge. Capable of implementing the most virtuous recycling, remediation, optimisation, and consumption reduction programmes. Capable of generating connectivity between enterprises, institutions and citizens, as well as recreating imaginaries. The complex apparatus of design culture is dedicated to preservation: a new step in that "longer history of planet imaginaries"[36] which, in its best manifestations (from Crystal Palace to Malevič's planets), has always been primarily political: breaching walls and breaking through the dimensions of the world. Today it appears to be more of an ascetic practice: the practice of a naturalist overcome by the ungovernable nature of his study objects. This was the typical position of early modernity: burdened by terror, sadness, and archaic instincts (if it is not too provocative and ungenerous to say so)—but also optimistic about triggering radical changes in behaviour, posing crucial questions in the public debate, and encouraging better conditions for everyone, and by so doing building a new universal meaning in a society that perceived the fall of twentieth-century universalisms. This too is a strong feature of modernity influencing contemporary anxieties.

It's easy to scoff at the mystic aspects that pander to our fears and anxieties and prompt us to "ally with other protagonists of the universe". To scorn positions that would like to be radical, but are instead prudent, democratic, and progressive. That swim against the tide of our more usual concerns. That lack the lucid irony that still inspires other voices. The mocking voice of Magnus Enzensberger, for example: "Nearly everything we are unable to solve is worked out by other beings living on this planet without any apparent effort. Many lichens can easily live a thousand years. Bacteria solve the problem of reproduction, that many struggle to face, in the easiest way possible: they divide, and it's done. Birds navigate by measuring the height of the sun, the polarisation of light, and the Earth's magnetic field. Butterflies have an incredible sense of smell".[37] In any case, we should be careful not to underestimate *Homo sapiens*. Enzensberger illustrates the limits of our power to know, imagine, control, and eliminate risks, uncertainties, and fears. As once emphasised by Alfonso Berardinelli, Enzensberger's irony follows and records the irony of facts. It is a good guide to understanding how the first half of the euphoric and traumatic fifties, and the first two decades of the twenty-first century, are more alike than the sixty years between these two periods. The topics of illness and survival are intertwined. Even the latter appears to be above all the survival of certain words: design, nature, survival. Although, of course, there was no Anthropocene to fuel our sense of guilt in the fifties.

The Sick Body Cared For by Design

The sick body and its neuroses act as a transit channel between space and design. Design variously medicates the sick body by adopting solutions that are either amazing and awe-inspiring or rapid, conventional, and insufficient. Ultimately, it always becomes the grand illusion of the medication of space: the long parabola towards hygienism, the desire for a healthy, ordered world where we can reduce the sources of our suffering, listed by Freud in 1929 as the overwhelming forces of nature, inadequate institutions, and the fragility of the body.[38]

The body is fragile; it falls sick. Design tackles this fragility, as it (for example) did tuberculosis in the early twentieth century: the algid example of Paimo's sanatorium, perhaps the most famous example, remains a place of pilgrimage for those who wish to understand the Finnish humanisation of modernism.[39] A hundred years earlier in the nineteenth century, cholera broke out in a world already globalised by the movement of military troops and goods—one in which epidemics not only caused the death of hundreds of thousands, but also changed the structure of society. Changes in the structure of society led to countless religious and pagan rites. At the time, hygienists, doctors, and engineers undid and redid the city in a titanic effort to fight this illness (which was tackled on another front by John Snow, Filippo Pacini, and Robert Koch)—but not without accurately describing the conditions.[40] Cholera is an illness that wounds, mutilates, lacerates, and ultimately kills the body. The sick body becomes an unfamiliar, foreign body to be segregated and hidden. The violent intrusion of the illness into the individual and social body merges with the malignancy that leads to death. The sick body is a threatening body, cared for through segregation: leper colonies, *cordons sanitaires*, militarisation (even if the military is the primary vector of disease transmission); self-defence groups ready to ward off foreigners, strangers, and vagabonds. At the end of the nineteenth century, medical surveys rewrote urban space based on the sick body.[41]

In the introduction to her most recent study, Beatriz Colomina writes that "modernity was driven by illness".[42] The engine of modern architecture was not a heroic, shiny, functional machine, but "a languid fragile body suspended outside daily life in a protective cocoon of new technologies and geometries".[43] Colomina encourages us to consider the intimate link between space and illness and imagine all the actors involved as patients: architects, clients, theorists, critics, and workers. What does it mean to make the sick (body) the key focus of design? This question is still pertinent today, given the current situation in which the body is wounded and deformed by new illnesses; obesity, Alzheimer's, cardiac diseases, solitude, and frustrations that maintain opaque and superimposed boundaries with clinical depression. These illnesses continue to inspire design ideas from *therapeutic design* to *stress researchers*.[44] Design's task is always to fight illness, anxiety, existential disorientation, and malaise, and to explain the ways that space helps to generate or reduce damage to the body and psyche. "A city is good if it counteracts social stress".[45] This approach is called *Neuro-Urbanism*, a

dreadful neologism. This version of urban planning takes into account the pathologies associated with stress; it is as optimistic as the old hygienism, but its design results are stimulated by a much more modest common sense.[46]
What is required to limit contemporary stress and defuse modern pathologies? Different ways to use the same places; the freedom to employ space in one's own way; a density of individuals, actions, and meanings. A measured density, because too much is as harmful as too little. We need to use bicycles (only those who can, obviously). These are the recipes provided by stress researchers to contain the anxieties of contemporary urban life. They are very few when compared to the luminous "spider-leg" architectures of modernism, to the devices aimed at overcoming twenty-first-century agoraphobia,[47] and to modern hygienism—both the rough-mannered hygienism that destroys the city and the hygienism that instead focuses on a healthy, athletic, and irremediably young body. An example of this latter kind is the insertion of the *Downtown Athletic Club* in the heart of New York's Financial District in 1931; it appears to be a locker room the size of a skyscraper, a "definitive manifestation of those metaphysics – at once spiritual and carnal – that protect the American male against the corrosion of adulthood".[48] This movement was taking place at the time European totalitarianisms were revealing the perverse relationship between the body and political ideology, each chained to the other, as reported by the young Emmanuel Lévinas in his courageous, argumentative and extremely lucid text entitled "*Quelques réflexions sur la philosophie de l'hitlérisme*".[49]
Compared to hygienism, modernism, and medical, social, and political ideologies, the practices that challenge the anxiety of the contemporary city are quite small: kitchen gardens, bicycles, and walking. In the meantime, the concept of the *Healthy City* has exploded. The medicalisation of space influenced professions and policies invested in the reconfiguration of the land and transportation; their main focus was the need to ensure health and wellbeing in a time of ageing and chronic illnesses. However, the field of action was enormous. It included the provision of equipment, capillary services, and assistance; new accessibility measures inside and outside the home; the creation of unbroken, branching, comfortable, and dedicated pathways; the upgrading of the size, measurements, and costs of heritage buildings; the restructuring of socio-sanitary services; the provision of home-based health services; the facilitation of forms of sharing; and the management of the effects on real estate investments. Cities became aware of the importance

of health as a collective asset, became capable of implementing policies to improve health; that is, policies encouraging citizens to lead an active life. Efforts a little like those Neutra's rich, learned client, Lovell, used to write about in the *Los Angeles Times* in the fifties when he suggested that we should go to bed early, exercise extensively, and eat well. In short, suggestions that made sense, that were destined for a level of structural imperfection, for contradictions generated by best intentions. A coerced effort by the body was to our advantage; so much so that, a few years ago, an interesting exhibition by the Canadian Centre of Architecture (meaningfully entitled "Imperfect Health")[50] illustrated an extensive study of this society obsessed with wellness and ready to insert the idea of physical, biological, social, and cultural well-being into the *Healthy City* concept. The idea was embodied in technical, methodical directives, accompanied by a new, subtly moralistic philosophy (*healthism*) built once again with individual, responsible awareness of the body at its hub.[51]

There are countless ways in which design cures and has cured the body. By projecting it in space, as in the organic analogy; by reconciling its ambivalence with old and new protocols that refer to codes as well as normalising and indicating simple categories: organisms to be healed, labour to be employed, the unconscious to be freed. Design cures the body by acting on space; by disembowelling, cleaning, bringing air, water and light, by organising pathways, and by disciplining uses. Its action combines space and body or merges body and space. Space renders manifest the presence of the body and its condition as a healthy or sick body shaped by neuroses or desire. Today, the topic of a healthy space, a healthy city, has regained a strong physical and political connotation. Roads, squares, neighbourhoods, and cities are healthy. They are spaces in which individuals are protected from illnesses; spaces filled with all kinds of vegetal essences and scales.

Who Do We Choose to Help?

Neutra's way forward undoubtedly appears more refined than those of the contemporary *Healthy City* because the latter are less direct and deterministic. But the problem remains: how can we cure the body by addressing it, signifying it, capturing the tension between what it brings with it and what it has lost (health, identity, sexuality, strength, and youth) and, at the same time, turn physical space into something material, stable, and heavy? How can we avoid overly hasty, conventional and insufficient answers:

the kitchen gardens, bicycles, and walks? How can we tackle the political dimension of *urban suffering* as outlined by Saraceno?[52] These are not technical questions. They involve the meaning of design; design that deals with the body by transforming space, by embracing the uniqueness of every condition and, at the same time, acknowledging the contingencies qualifying that condition and making it plural.[53] Treating the body is an operation that, precisely in this transfer (from singular to plural), has a *public value*. This is why Neutra's projects, commissioned by the cinematographic world in California—and acidly commented on by Zevi—are so interesting: they talk about the neuroses of that period and help to delineate public issues free from fake morality.

The questions posed by the curators of the "Imperfect Health" exhibition organised by the CCA are still crucial: do we live in a health-obsessed society? Is health an individual responsibility or a public concern? Do architectural types mirror the specialised needs of medicine? Is *healthism* our new religion? Do we all share the same ideas about health and illness? And finally: how do space and architecture reflect the requirements of medicine? There's yet another question that triggers other questions, one that is at the root of this issue: who do we choose to help? In the end, this is the million-dollar question. Neutra was sincerely interested in the repression and sublimation of libido—the Freudian mechanism that inspired him to decrypt symptoms and imagine spaces. Contemporary stress researchers only vaguely examine an unwell public: one that ages, falls sick, is depressed, suffers the competitiveness and the intense frenetic rhythms of a world increasingly lacking in gentleness and solidarity. Nevertheless, stress researchers maintain that it is possible to improve conditions in an appropriate environment. The designers "of survival", should we wish to include them, are careful to pander to conventional wisdom: they look at humans and lichens together. The issue, however, requires more radical formulas: how does a society provide protection? Who do we choose, consciously or unconsciously, to protect? How can we reinterpret this desire for a healthy, ordered world where we can reduce the sources of our suffering? How can we turn all this into the manifestation of a social justice that becomes spatial? And, finally, what are the needs and basic desires—protection from illnesses, safety, a sense of belonging—of those who are relegated outside the circle of the ones we decide to protect? Or, put more clearly, and using the words of Judith Butler (and Adorno), how can we have a moral approach in periods of precariousness?[54]

Notes

1   Richard Neutra, *Survival Through Design*,
    New York: Oxford University Press,
    1954: 117
2   John Huston (directed by), *The Maltese
    Falcon*, 101', USA, Warner Bros, 1941
3   Robert Banham, *Scenes in America
    Deserta*, Utah: Gibbs Smith Publishers,
    1982
4   Neutra, *Survival Through Design*, cit.
5   Ivi: VII
6   "Organically oriented design could, we
    hope, combat the chance character of the
    surrounding scene", Ivi: 4
7   Bruno Zevi, *Richard Neutra*, Milano:
    Il Balcone, 1954; Thomas Hines,
    *Richard Neutra and the search for modern
    architecture: A biography and history*,
    New York: Oxford University Press,
    1982; Manfred Sack, *Richard Neutra*,
    Zürich: Verlag für Architektur, 1992;
    the three monographs edited by Willy
    Boesiger: *Richard Neutra 1923–1949.
    Buildings and Projects*, (Boesiger ed.),
    Zürich: Verlag, 1950; *Richard Neutra
    1950–1960. Buildings and Projects*,
    (Boesiger ed.), Zürich: Verlag, 1960;
    *Richard Neutra 1961–1966. Buildings
    and Projects*, (Boesiger ed.), Zürich:
    Verlag, 1966; Sylvia Lavin, *Form Follows
    Libido*, Cambridge Massacchusetts:
    MIT Press, 2004; Beatriz Colomina,
    X-Ray Architecture, Zürich: Lars Müller
    Publishers, 2019, 45–52
8   Richard Neutra, "How Become an
    Architect?" *Journal of Architectural
    Education (1947-1974)*, vol. 15, no. 1,
    (1960): 19–20. *JSTOR*, www.jstor.org/
    stable/1424129 Neutra's personal life also
    affected his ideas: his own depression,
    his son's disability, his ongoing dialogue
    with Freud, and his meetings with the
    psychiatrist Karl Menninger.
9   Neutra's essays clearly betray this
    penchant to study himself, his feelings
    and his childhood. This is a long but very
    significant excerpt:
    "Early in life we spend much time floored
    baby-fashion, perplexed, most curious.
    As a two- and three-year-old, I often sat
    on the parquet of my parent's apartment,
    studying the raised, splintery grain of the
    worn hardwood and the warped boards.

The cracks between the boards were filled
with a compact something which I liked
to dig out with my fingers. To grown-ups
the floor is distant. Had they stooped
to examine what I produced from this
quiet resting place of open parquetry
joints, they would have called it dirt.
Magnification could have shown it to be
a teeming microbiotic world. I tested it
by the toddler's ancient test – put it into
the mouth and found it 'no good'.
Strange as it may seem, my first
impressions of architecture were largely
gustatory. I liked the bottler-like
wallpaper adjoining my bed pillow, and
the polished brass hardware of my toy
cupboard. It must have been then and
there that I developed an unconscious
preference for flawlessly smooth surfaces
that would stand the tongue test, the
most exacting of tactile investigation[s],
and for less open-jointed, and also more
resilient flooring. I recall, that scantily
dressed or naked as I was, I became
uneasily aware of the surface on which I
set [sat] and moved.
It was then, also, that I first experienced
the sensation of towering height by
looking upward to the carved top of a
Victorian dresser. I was more awed and
impressed than, later, [by] the gigantic
columns that support the vaults of the
cathedral of Milan or the roof of the
Temple at Luxor.
The idea of shelter is associated in my
mind with a feeling that took root in me
during those days. Our parlour ceiling
was uncomfortably high, and so I used to
sit and play under the grand piano. The
low headroom under our piano provided
me the cosiest place I knew … At night
there were dark, inaccessible, mysterious
spaces – such as that frightening area [at
the] back of the olive-green upholstered
love seat, placed 'catty-corner' into the
room. I still shudder at the memory. And
I still loathe the waste of space behind
furniture.
Those many childhood experiences
taught unspoken lessons in appreciation
of space, texture, light, and shade, the
smell of carpets, the warmth of wood,
and the coolness of the stone hearth in
front of our kitchen stove.

Later our college lectures on architecture never touched on such basic sensory experiences, or on the subtle relationship between physical structures and man's nervous behaviour."
Neutra, *Survival Through Design*, cit.: 25–26

10 Neutra's writings are housed in the Online Archive of California (Oac California Digital Library) https://oac.cdlb.org.ask.admin; Edward T. Hall: *The Hidden dimension*, New York: Anchor Books Editions, 1969 (first ed. 1966) https://www.academia.edu/5668023/Edward_T._Hall-_The_Hidden_Dimension

11 Gilles Deleuze, "Cinq propositions sur la psychanalyse" (1973) in *L'île deserte et autres textes*, Paris: Les Éditions de Minuit, 2002. Translation from the Italian edition: "Cinque proposizioni sulla psicanalisi", in *L'isola deserta e altri scritti*, Torino: Einaudi, 2007: 348–356

12 Lavin, *Form Follows Libido*, cit.

13 Zevi, *Richard Neutra*, cit.: 7. These words are written in the tenth volume of the collection entitled "Architetti del Movimento Moderno" edited by Lodovico Belgiojoso, Enrico Peressuti, and Ernesto Rogers. It begins with a very critical passage: "The inhibitory Calvinist concept, stripped of the architecture Adolf Loos revealed to his students, in the impetus of unbridled faith in the spiritual and civic value of figurative simplicity, is ill-suited to the professional activity performed for the cinematographic world of California" p. 7. It continued with the phrase cited above. This very harsh opening was counterbalanced by a much softer closure: "against the miraculism of the genius [Neutra] proposed a literary alternative; he impersonated its virtues and testified that being educated does not exclude the experience of poetic grace". Ivi: 36

14 Allison & Peter Smithson, *Without Rhetoric. An Architectural Aesthetic. 1955-1972*, Massachussetts: MIT Press, Cambridge, 1973: 26. The longer excerpt: "Neutra's houses, as they exist in photographs, are so polished, so perfect, as to seem impossible to achieve:

as if their builders all wore white gloves and tabi and had their bath-house hut erected as the first building on site in the Japanese manner: As if their owners never had an unpresentable moment or laid down a pair of sun glasses. The photographs have a kind of de-materialised glamour, almost that of soap and toilet paper advertisements (although which came first is difficult to tell) that is specially, even uniquely American, rooted no doubt on the standards upheld by the pioneer women of "The Little House" stories. This American cargo-cult architecture of technology is un-exportable. It is a much lesser thing that is exportable". See also Matthias Brunner, "Richard Neutra's Ambiguous Relationship to Luxury", *Arts*, no. 7(4), (2018), 75; https://doi.org/10.3390/arts7040075

15 Sack, *Richard Neutra*, cit.: 11

16 Boesiger, *Richard Neutra Buildings and Projects 1923–1959*, cit.

17 Lavin, *Form follows libido*, cit.: 48

18 Michel Foucault, "I rapporti di potere passano attraverso i corpi", in *Millepiani*, no. 9, Associazione culturale Mimesis, Milano, (1996): 9–17

19 Lavin, *Form follows libido*, cit.: 73

20 Neutra, *Survival Through Design*, cit.

21 Lavin, *Form follows libido*, cit.: 73

22 "If architecture is an affair of many senses, the stage assigned to it, space itself, is in fact also a multisensorial product which begins to evolve for us while we are still in the uterus. The prenatal experiment of shelter, floating in the evenly warm liquid medium of the mother's womb, is a primary factor moulding our later relations to an outer world, and to the architectural compartments that we construct for our later life". Neutra, *Survival Through Design*, cit.: 156. Chapter 22 focuses exclusively on something he calls the "physiological concept of space", p. 149

23 "In the light of our discussion so far, we may attempt now to formulate the designer's professional task in terms of valid requirements of the human organism. He must attempt to strike a happy medium between those psychological imperatives that

are the constants of life, on the one hand, and on the other, the acquired responses, which by his professional judgment he finds possible to include in a wholesomeness honestly. If physicians take such a humane oath, the designer must too". Neutra, *Survival Through Design*, cit.: 325. Neutra recalls Douglas N. Morgan, "Psychology and Art Today: A Summary and Critique", *The Journal of Esthetics and Art Criticism*, (December 1950). This is the only direct reference to the field of psychology.

24 Zevi, *Richard Neutra*, cit.: 72

25 Brunner, *Richard Neutra's Ambiguous Relationship to Luxury*, cit.; Colomina, *X-Ray Architecture*, cit.

26 Lavin, *Form Follows Libido*, cit.: 40 et foll.

27 Ivi: 40

28 Ivi: 42

29 "An environment she could love so much it would make her homesick". Ivi: 42

30 Sylvia Lavin, *Form Follows Libido*, Cambridge Massachusetts: MIT Press, 2004: 42

31 Ivi: 42

32 Deleuze, "*Cinque proposizioni sulla psicanalisi*", cit.: 348

33 Paola Antonelli (ed.), *Broken Nature. Design Takes on Human Survival*, XXII International Exposition of the Milan Triennale, Milan: Electa, 2019

34 See Rosi Braidotti and Maria Hlavajova (eds. by), *Posthuman Glossary*, London: Bloomsbury Academic, 2018

35 Antonelli, *Broken Nature. Design Takes on Human Survival*, cit.: 27

36 James Graham, *Climates: Architecture and the Planetary Imaginary*, Zürich: Lars Müller Publishers, 2016

37 Magnus Enzensberger, *Panopticon: Twenty Ten-minute Essays*, London – New York: Seagull Books, 2018, translation from the Italian edition *Panopticon. Venti saggi da leggere in dieci minuti*, Torino: Einaudi, 2019: 25

38 Sigmund Freud, *Civilisation and its Discontents* (1930), New York: W.W. Norton & Company, 2005

39 "The main purpose of the building is to function as a medical instrument … One of the basic prerequisites for healing is to provide complete peace … The layout of the rooms is based on the limited forces of the patient, lying in bed. The colour of the ceiling is chosen to convey tranquillity, light sources are outside the patient's field of vision, heating is directed towards his feet and water comes noiselessly out of the tap, so that no-one disturbs his neighbour". Alvar Alto cited in Peter Reed, *Alvar Aalto, 1898-1976*, Milano: Electa, 1998: 17

40 Axel Munthe, *Letters from a Mourning City: Naples, Autumn, 1884 (1887)*, ed. Create Space Independent Publishing Platform, 2016; Frank Snowden, *Naples at the Time of Cholera 1884–1911*, Cambridge University Press, 2010. Cholera struck the city of Naples in 1884 causing 7,000 deaths—half of all the deaths in Italy.

41 A health study performed in Italy in 1899—illustrated in a letter dated 11 January by the Ministry of Health and sent to the provincial doctors of the Kingdom—contained information regarding the detailed reconstruction of the country through the severe lens of hygienist doctors. Guido Zucconi, *La città contesa*, Milano: Jaca Book, 1989 and Carla Giovannini, *Risanare le città. L'utopia igienista alla fine dell'Ottocento*, Milano: Franco Angeli, 1996

42 Beatriz Colomina, *X-Ray Architecture*, Zürich: Lars Müller Publishers, 2019: 11

43 Colomina, *X-Ray Architecture*, cit.: 11

44 This is the definition Mazdla Adli uses to describe himself in his book. See "A city is good if it counteracts social stress", interview in *Topos*, monographic issue: *Healing Landscapes*, no. 166, (2019): 38–39

45 Ivi

46 Here the big difference with literature is that it often deals with the most despairing and complex conditions of individual prostration and economic and institutional trajectories. See, for example, Michel Houllebecq, *Serotonin*, London: William Heinemann, 2019

47 Anthony Vidler, *Art, Architecture and Anxiety in Modern Culture*, Cambridge Massachusetts: MIT Press, 2000

48 Rem Koolhaas, *Delirious New York*, New York: Monacelli Press, 1994: 157

49 Emmanuel Lévinas, *Quelques réflexions*

sur la philosophie de l'hitlérisme, published in 1934 by Esprit. Lévinas argued that European philosophy, and the old liberalism with an idealist matrix that aimed to emancipate the body, were crushed by what he calls the "philosophy of Hitlerism"; a belief that nails the ego to the body and therefore to race and power, as well as to violence and intolerance. The ego cannot be free of the body: one cannot be "thrown" into the other, and every form of reappropriation of ego must pass through the consciousness of this bond. Heidegger, Lévinas' teacher (who had attended Heidegger's lessons in 1928 and 1929) was familiar with this "enchainment"; Levinas countered it with a Jewish culture of exodus which he had absorbed through an incessant dialogue with the Talmud and his experience of Hebraism. He pitted a culture of "evasion" against the "community of blood", enchainment, and oppression.

50 Giovanna Borasi and Mirko Zardini (eds.), *Imperfect Health. The Medicalization of Architecture*, Zürich: CCA – Lars Müller Publishers, 2012

51 Borasi and Zardini, "Demedicalize Architecture", in *Imperfect Health. The Medicalization of Architecture*, cit.: 15–37

52 The Italian psychiatrist Benedetto Saraceno has a much less consolatory position regarding the relationship between health and the city. He introduces the category of *urban suffering*. Saraceno shifts the paradigm of suffering and reduces the welfare theme to a nontrivial private and public dimension. "The urban adjective, referred to suffering, places the latter in a symbolic, tangible, inhabited, social, and visible context"—but removes it from a private dimension. Suffering is not the exclusive prerogative of the last among us: it involves illness, malaise, psychic discomfort, and exclusion. The city offers these individuals places where they can hide, survive, and have relationships. Recalling Ota de Leonardis, he maintains that "the subjective experience of suffering has a political statute". Saraceno radically reverses the approach behind the *Healthy City*: it is the city itself that

"produces collective vulnerability, but denies the collectivity of vulnerability", providing individual answers in a de-subjectivising form. The echoes of Franco Basaglia's battles regarding the treatment of mental health are evident here. Benedetto Saraceno, *Psicopolitica. Città salute migrazioni*, Roma: Derive Approdi, 2019, cit.: 32, 30, 9

53 The same position by Vittorio Lingiardi: "Senza mappe per questi territori. Essere cartografi delle sessualità oggi", in Lorena Preta (ed.), *Dislocazioni. Nuove forme del disagio psichico e sociale*, Milano: Mimesis, 2018: 19–28

54 Judith Butler, *Qu'est-ce qu'une vie bonne?*, Paris: Payot, 2014, translation from English of her acceptance speech on 11 September 2012 before being awarded the "Adorno Prize" and published initially in Le Monde, (September 28, 2012), entitled "Une morale, pour temps précaire".

THE BODY OPEN TO THE WORLD

Let there be writing, not about the body, but the body itself. Not bodihood, but the actual body. Not signs, images, or ciphers of the body, but still the body. This was once a program for modernity, no doubt already it no longer is.
Nancy, 2008[1]

Agricultural and Urban Parks in the Rift of the Eighties

Parc du Sausset: twenty-two hectares in the department of Seine-Saint-Denis, north of Paris, between the small towns of Aulnay-sous-Bois and Villepinte. A well-known project,[2] yet one somehow considered minor by the extensive literature on parks, gardens, and landscapes. In 1980, the General Council for the Department of Seine-Saint-Denis launched a competition to turn a vast, cultivated area into a public park. The competition specified that the agricultural landscape was to be protected, restored, and transformed into a park. Building was started in 1982 based on a design by Claire and Michel Corajoud. Michel's words will help us understand the features of the project: *"Je reste très sensible aux paysage de campagne … regarder la campagne, c'est éprouver et reprendre à son compte le sens du travail qui l'a produite: c'est saisir, dans son propre corps, une dynamique de réalisation: c'est trouver les lignes de partage, le seuils, les recouvrements successifs. C'est comprendre confusément l'histoire des générations qui se sont succédé et qui ont dressé cet draperie, sans toutefois réussir à vaincre les résistances du site, comme ce rocher qui en crève toujours la surface"*.[3]

Corajoud had a true passion for the rural landscape. In other passages he reiterates that he considers cultivated fields as important as lines on a piece of paper: "the writings of a place begin [in] the fields".[4] The graphemes that make up the multifaceted writing system of the French countryside are assigned to the stratified work of time, the presence of water, empty spaces, groups of trees, meadows, linear elements, rows, and hedges. And, primarily, to the fact that they are combined but do not alter the ductility and permeability of the landscape. So much so that *"il est toujours possible de passer où voir au travers de presque tout"*,[5] thereby signalling the antithesis of the urban. The traces of cultivation in the countryside are carefully studied in Parc du Sausset[6]: lines that carve the ground, that follow it along its altimetric curves and the openings of its horizons[7]; signs that display the measurements of the territory, its subdivisions, and their ability to evoke collective values, as well as their functional and semantic importance. Careful attention is likewise paid to the "vegetal scenes".[8] All this reveals a park both agricultural and urban, in debt to the French tradition of the *promenade*, reminiscent of Alphand and Abbot Laugier as well as to the rural countryside; an atypical combination, but not the only surprising element. The *bocage* system in the park was initially organised without cultivated plots, without flocks, without fences, without farmers, and without farms. Pierre Donadieu wrote about a "dis-agriculturised" countryside: fields equipped with benches, ready-made for improbable outings. Fields carefully tailored until someone decides to "re-agriculturise" them.[9] Donadieu's assessment is severe, almost sarcastic: the project "proposes rural images more like the ones dreamt by urban dwellers than the ones that existed [in that area]".[10]

Donadieu appears, however, to have ignored the topic tackled by this project, which is intended primarily to recompose, reconcile, and include all aspects of a vital world; to preserve resources that would generate resistance to the specialisation and impoverishment of the landscape. To include alterity. To keep diversity together. To stand against every sensorial approach to landscape, against remedial and reparatory approaches, against the overwriting of parts of theories, policies, and bureaucratic classifications. To remain close to the ground. To spy on its transformation. Corajoud used the word "conciliation" to explain all this. The park exemplifies the obstinate, almost naive intent to keep the rural, urban, and natural environment together. Without them overpowering one another. Without antagonism. The year Parc du Sausset was created, the Hungarian-born conceptual artist Agnes

Denes created a scornful version of the intensely anti-modern stance by creating her famous two-acre field just two blocks from the World Trade Centre: wheat grown on land worth 4.5 billion dollars.[11] In the universe of reconciliation that now appears to us as ironic, ethical, and anti-planning, agriculture occupied a highly respectable position.

Despite these warning signs, there was no inkling of the current explosion of excitement about urban agriculture in the eighties. The change in perspective (that the city can be understood if seen from the countryside) was triggered by Pierre Donadieu and his book *Campagnes Urbaines*, published twenty years ago.[12] However, this re-orientation slowly lost its forcefulness as it was disseminated and democratised in the countless constellations of communal gardens and vegetable patches: bit by bit, in little plots of land, in courtyards, on roofs, and on the ground around modernist buildings. The re-introduction of vegetable gardens in the city is the most popular form of contemporary *agrophilia*. It was celebrated everywhere—until it sparked disquieting images of cities made up of vegetable gardens, of the most democratic, most ductile urban material, the one most capable of satisfying the expectations of city inhabitants and administrators. They express a joyful, shared criticism of the bourgeois city, the industrial society, and the commercialisation and commoditisation of land. The pervasive presence of the vegetable garden creates an anti-modern and anti-progressive city. It involves actions by small groups: mutual benefit cooperatives created to produce and exchange, i.e., to pre-emptively limit the damage wrought by the isolation of every individual. However, despite the popularity of self-production and the enthusiasms and nightmares it causes, it also raises complicated questions regarding the management of productive processes. Just think of what its proliferation entails: economic, technical, biological, and water-based requirements suited to the consistency and quality of the terrain. Or the redesigning of space, exclusive uses, and shared practices, and the ensuing balance of forces, conflicts, and appropriations. It is not exactly clear who the protagonists of these productive cycles are, apart from the easy rhetoric referring to their benefits for aged individuals. It would be interesting to study how long vegetable gardens will resist and endure in our cities.

Parc du Sausset was built before the season of urban countrysides, *agrophilia*, and vegetable gardens. It is an unusual, disturbing rural park; meticulously designed, with benches in the fields. It can be considered a model of the sophisticated French tradition of the landscape combining rural fringes, suburban settlements, and infrastructures with good ecological sensitivities. A continuously evolving place in which users can perceive and enjoy the evolutionary dynamics of the landscape.[13]

The competition for Parc de la Villette was also launched in 1982.[14] It is considered one of the most important competitions, if not *the* most important competition, of the second half of the twentieth century. With Burle Mark as president of an authoritative jury, Rem Koolhaas and Bernard Tschumi fought a final battle worthy of a superhero epic. Together with Jacques Derrida, Tschumi won the competition. Their project became the manifesto for "deconstructivism" in architecture. Competitions are like gymnasiums.

They are incredible experimental fields in which to compare several genetically different spatial ideas: *spaces of freedom, creativity and flexibility* for Bernard Tschumi; licentious and frivolous, the space shifted into the field of events. *Analogical space* for Peter Eisenman, who focuses on conceptualising and abstracting interpretations within a sophisticated, combinatory art; he works on offhandedness, pursuing the project along repressed traces that resurface in Freudian analysis (again through the diagram concept developed by Derrida, the real philosophical deity of this whole affair).[15] *Spaces of rhythms and frequencies* for Koolhaas: an approach that owes its conception to the CIAM grid, the extreme echo of a functionalism all too hastily given up for dead.[16] Likewise, the grid is used in Melun-Sénart to frame territorial regularity on the one hand and programmatic spaces on the other. It is a new social order, the result of "futurological research" leading to spaces saturated with traces and intentions; with axes and bands that avoid narrative sequences; based on the repetition of functional units; "fields of experimentation for utopian practices".

This is not the place to revive the complex story of that competition, nor that of the divergent results. However, I shall say this: the projects for Parc de la Villette provide an exemplary reinterpretation of the links between politics and the economy during the rise of an aggressive and powerful neo-liberalism. They nimbly leapfrogged the twentieth century, prefiguring an urban universe characterised by processes, programmes, and flows. The prophetic nature assigned to them is linked to the absence of any functional and compositional tension in redesigning places believed to be capable of acting as accelerators of a new metropolitan culture; almost as if to prefigure a different social ethos embodied in urban space, with all its associated ideological tools of seduction, creativity and experimentation. Tools learnt during the struggles of the sixties and seventies and rejected, weakened, in the glitzy *cities of pleasure* that followed. Or rather, within "*le nouvelle esprit du capitalisme*", recalling the ambitious and fittingly famous study by Boltanski and Chiapello,[17] who, referring directly to Weber's even more famous study,[18] piece together the re-articulation of practices and discursive formations implemented by capital in the uncertain decades of the late twentieth century to support and legitimise a new hegemony. Boltanski and Chiapello narrate the transformation of a different imaginary: that of company management, in which the apology of change, risk, and mobility impetuously takes over.

Bodies of Pleasure / Disposing of the Body

Parc du Sausset and Parc de la Villette are obviously not comparable, but what I wish to emphasise here is that there are many different ways that we refer to the body of pleasure. For Clair and Michel Corajoud, a park refers to a body open to the world, a body that enjoys the world; in addition to enjoying the world, it not only acts, suffers, and works within it, but also has knowledge of it. We live and act in space through our bodies. The experience of the *promenades continues* is movement. Movement of the body in space; movement that dilates points of observation and endlessly rewrites the relationships linking bodies to the landscape; movement that continuously redefines the horizon, where "*le ciel et la terre se touchent*".[19] Corajoud considers it to be a physical trait, the essence of the landscape itself. Walks, gazes, movements, horizons: even the benches, simultaneously insignificant and presumptuous, take on a different meaning. The body literally escapes into pleasure, aspires only to come out, to place itself in the gentleness of the spaces, in the intoxication of light, in the way in which shadows either blur or fall crisply on the ground.

Corajoud seems to ask: when facing a place that moves and unsettles us, how often do we say: "I am here"? I am here in front of this meadow, this lake. I am this meadow, this lake. I am this place. The body expands and literally escapes; dilates, incorporates a space that is both internal and external—as it does when dancing. It is no longer just the body that is in space; space is also in the body. The body is here. It is around it that things are arranged, "as if in relation to a sovereign". Paths and space cross in the body, in this "small utopian kernel".[20]

In an excerpt of a later essay, Corajoud uses these words to describe the body of pleasure:

"You will undoubtedly have gone one day to read in the woods, stretching your legs out in the sun with your body in the shade: I think this is an archetype associated with the feeling of wellbeing and happiness".[21]

This is similar to Bernardo Secchi's listing of the physical and emotional states of sitting on the ground in Piazza del Campo in Siena:

"Who has never tried to look at the square for a long time, to see how the shadows and sun move during the seasons and the way they fill the various corners; who hasn't remained seated on the ground in this square, sheltered from the wind, and appreciated the soft warmth of the bricks and the square's inclination; who hasn't looked at the simple ways in which the pattern of the paving helps water drain away from this immense area on a rainy day …".[22]

What's important is the universe of light and its repertoire of different possibilities: the consistency of the shadows, the reflections, the effect of mist, light rain, or fog, the nuanced colours at certain times of day and in certain weather conditions. What's important is to enjoy the air. And, obviously, the consistency of the ground, its softness, its "flawlessly smooth surfaces",[23] its unhindered continuity, and the sun-kissed warmth of the bricks in Piazza del Campo. What's important is the granularity of the materials, their ability to let water or sand drain away. Very physical conditions which, in the words of John Dewey, intensify vitality.[24] The body of pleasure invents, recomposes, replicates, and dilates itself. It merges with what gives it pleasure. Most landscape projects refer to a hedonist body that enjoys its relationship with nature. One extreme case (although this is a decidedly imbalanced comparison) is Zheng Bo's performance in which enjoyment becomes sexual enjoyment, a violent and anthropophagous eroticism that explores an eco-queer perspective.[25]

There is an active dimension to the body of pleasure that is crucial: the fact that the body is interwoven with the world represents continuous birth, agitation, unease, pain, and joy.[26] The body of pleasure is a body absorbed by its own ability to change, passing from a consistency governed by social, cultural, and technical norms to a much freer form. Disposing of space means disposing of one's body. What these projects tell us is that the space of the world belongs to the body, in the same way that flesh belongs to the body. Being in the space of the world, and enjoying it, is the opposite of the body being isolated in the world and considered an object. The condition is physical and material before it is aesthetic. This condition represents the power of the body to act: the body is illuminated, invested by the world; it is different kinds of "affection" and this increases its power to act.[27] It is the power of the material finiteness of the body.

How is design related to the dilated body, open to the world of pleasure? Not in a functionalist manner (the park as a place of *loisir*), because bodies are always affected by specific circumstances, and functionalism is unable to govern specificities (in the words of Gabriele Pasqui, unable to govern the radical pluralism of life forms).[28] Bodies are the transit of the forces that pass through them: light, water, fog, breeze, warmth, etc. They are places of meetings, both good and bad, which thereby either increase or decrease their power.[29] The world passes through these meetings: Spinoza wrote that "to preserve itself the body needs a great many other bodies".[30] A political dimension echoes in the body that exists together with other human bodies—but not only with human bodies. A design dimension echoes in the fact that we live in the city in the encumbrance of our bodies.

The Parisian competition of 1982 was, as mentioned earlier, a gymnasium, a field of experimentation where a different idea of the body of pleasure was implemented. Bernard Tschumi[31] believes that pleasure and enjoyment, too, are expressions of the virus of the informal nourishing the spirit of late capitalism. Lightness, creativity, flexibility: Huizinga's *homo ludens* resurfaces in the urban scene, bringing with it a concept of freedom that dissolves the ordinary world.

"First and foremost all play is a voluntary activity. Play to order is no longer play: it could at best be but a forcible imitation of it. …. The first main characteristic of play … is in fact freedom. …. Inside the circle of the game the laws and customs of ordinary life no longer count. We are different and do things differently."[32]

Productive capitalist logic is jeopardised by the use of play elements. Play elements are superimposed on it like an ornament, and, in the process, denied. Here too the functionalism of the scenic and narrative units is overcome in favour of a radicality that introduces the sacredness of another order.[33] Huizinga is softened: his play element is held within the limits of a meagre, measured time and space. There are no out-of-control parties. Subversive positions are declared and ultimately incarnate the "new (neoliberalist) spirit of capitalism".[34] A reversal that deserves to be emphasised.

Historical and political Italian culture initially ridiculed Huizinga but later idolatrised him for his free play idea, which became popular again when bodies, places, and politics were combined into an unusual mix in the eighties.[35] Urban design was fully aware of this "crossroads" and nestled into its ambiguities, tangibly taking advantage of the possibilities and openings it provided; for example, by using the image of the playground, as repeatedly exploited in the competition for Parc de la Villette. One could object that it was an easy but very clear metaphor that outlined a space filled with and emptied of bodies, of relationships between bodies seeking each other, ignoring each other, and taking pleasure in their associations, contiguities, dislocations and superimpositions. The *playground* is a space made up of empty spaces ready for play, of once-meaningful spaces now reduced to markers. They are highly symbolic spaces, even if we are not overly familiar with how the play element takes place there.[36] Vidler refers to Alice in her repeatedly cited croquet game with the Queen—a game in which there are no fixed rules and everything constantly moves haphazardly. It is a generous and recurring reference, not so much during the period when Vidler wrote the original edition of *The Architectural Uncanny. Essays in the Modern Unhomely* (published in 1992), but when Tschumi was designing his projects. During this period, which challenged reason and its methods, the croquet game with the Queen became a crucial metaphor. A few decades on, it is obvious that this uncertainty no longer describes the crisis of reason but rather an element of play which, in its own way, astute and opportunistic, expresses a combination of politics, the city, and the body.

Whatever Happened to the Debate on Landscape and its Happy Bodies?

Parc du Sausset and Parc de la Villette were rooted in the eighties, when many people were discussing the features of a new, freer, decentred, polymorphic, and ungraspable age. What could be better than a big public park, regardless of whether it was agricultural or urban? The two projects satisfied this commitment to promoting forms radically opposite to the body of pleasure. The former involved rediscovering the ideals of transparency between harmony, sign, signifier, and the increased power of the body; between the design of the terrain and the "great many ways" in which a body is continuously regenerated by its encounter with other bodies.[37] The latter consisted of dissociating these bonds and inventing new ones, of creating clashes and provoking breakages and dissonances. On the one hand, the body of pleasure closely linked to the space of the park, calm and disquieting under the surface; on the other, bonds challenged by the use of empty space and solved by action.

The two parks provide an excellent picture of the rift that divided a before and an after:[38] the rift of the eighties. In Gramsci's words, we could say it was a shift towards a different hegemonic order, in which the language of previous decades—with their attempts to achieve authenticity and self-organisation as well as to oppose all hierarchies—is reversed and used to promote new forms of control. Within that shift, a complex naturalisation process of the critical practices of a different social order takes place. What had been considered subversive a little earlier was rapidly adopted and canonised. Some believe it was the shift from Fordism to post-Fordism.[39] For architects and urban planners it was the ultimate change in the urban discourse.[40]

The season of landscape, illustrated in vast, undisciplined, and extensive literature, appears to paradoxically draw strength from this shift. In the rift of the eighties, at the height of that season, positions multiply, bringing together the Atlas of emotions,[41] Sloterdijk big greenhouse,[42] multiple projects and gardens, as well as the relentless adoption of increasingly fluid, smoothed, and vague environments where groups of individuals are portrayed in bucolic, pastoral situations, even when they are sitting on the wild banks of the Ruhr or a vast snow-covered plain, as in Peter Bialobrezeshi's photographs.[43] Everywhere the body merges with the landscape. The ecumene: adherence to, harmony with, and immersion in the outside world;[44] something "almost religious"[45] where onlookers seem to move away from their own substance. A loss of sense of self, more similar to ecstasy than to bewilderment. A feeling that simultaneously exposes the body to separateness, unknowability, and enigma.[46]

Flowing like masses of liquid, there came wave after wave of studies on the landscape: architectural and ecological, aesthetic, philosophical, culturalist; on concerns regarding the Anthropocene, on the attraction to new technological landscapes. On the metaphor of the garden: a good place for holistic visions of nature. Or on abandoned spaces that became openings leading towards the future: spaces of survival. All the way to the celebration of the casual and contingent: a landscape that exposes itself quickly and immediately disappears. Landscape design absorbed everything, but in an increasingly weary manner, and displaying greater worn frivolity. One could ask: what happened after the dissolution of landscape cultures and the subcultures that straddled the rift of the late twentieth century by prolonging it? By filling it with happy bodies, variations mixed with aesthetic and conservatory approaches? How did a series of so many landscape designs develop reflections about the body-space-politics merger highlighted so well by the La Villette project? Can this story, with its aporias and vagueness, be critically reviewed by making the body (the body of pleasure) the focus of said review? Its "Right You Are! (If You Think You So)"[47] that assembled everything, and held everything—including the advantage of imprecision, should we wish to cite Corajoud once again.[48]

Notes

1 Jean-Luc Nancy, *Corpus*, New York: Fordham University Press, 2008: 9

2 Isotta Cortesi, *Il parco pubblico. 1985–2000*, Milano: Federico Motta, 2000: 154

3 Michel Corajoud, *Le paysage, c'est l'endroit où le ciel et la terre se touchent*, Actes sud, ENSP, 2010: 15–16. Many of Corajoud's essays and books are available at http://corajoudmichel.nerim.net/

4 Michel Corajoud, "Tutto è patrimonio" in Carmen Andriani (ed.), *Il patrimonio e l'abitare*, Roma: Donzelli, 2010, 37–44, cit: 40

5 Michel Corajoud, "L'Horizon, Interview", for *Face* on 5 March 2004 at http://corajoudmichel.nerim.net/10-textes/01a-horizon.htm

6 The emphasis on writing, lexically merged with the problem of the intelligibility of space, was very strong in landscape schools in France and Switzerland: the Geneva Model was adopted by designers and critics such as Giairo Daghini, Georges Descombes, Riccardo Mariani, Bruno Reichlin, and even André Corboz, who used the key concept of palimpsest. For several years, the Geneva Model was developed by the *Centre de la Recherche sur la Rénovation Urbaine* (CRR). This took place more or less in the eighties; contacts with the Italian school were not limited to reciprocal contributions in architectural journals. Towards the end of the decade Secchi taught in Geneva as a visiting professor and Gregotti often contributed essays and designs.

7 Michel Courajoud, "Un chemin du Parc du Sausset", in *Le paysage, c'est l'endroit où le ciel et la terre se touchent*, Actes sud, ENSP, 2010, 47–48, originally published in *Pour*, no. 89, (May-June 1983) entitled "*Le paysage, une façon de vivre*".

8 Cortesi, *Il parco pubblico*, cit: 152. See also the chapter "Paesaggi produttivi" in Gianni Celestini, *Agire con il paesaggio*, Roma: Aracne, 2018: 71–83

9 Pierre Donadieu, *Campagne urbane*, Roma: Donzelli, 2006: 151

10 *Ibidem*

11 *Wheatfield— A Confrontation: Battery Park Landfill, Downtown Manhattan*. From the artist's website: "After months of preparations, in May 1982, a 2-acre wheat field was planted on a landfill in lower Manhattan, two blocks from Wall Street and the World Trade Center, facing the Statue of Liberty. Two hundred truckloads of dirt were brought in and 285 furrows were dug by hand and cleared of rocks and garbage. The seeds were sown by hand and the furrows covered with soil. The field was maintained for four months, cleared of wheat smut, weeded, fertilized and sprayed against mildew fungus, and an irrigation system set up. The crop was harvested on August 16 and yielded over 1000 pounds of healthy, golden wheat. Planting and harvesting a field of wheat on land worth $4.5 billion created a powerful paradox". http://agnesdenesstudio.com/works7.html Andy Goldsworthy's equally famous photograph shows a woman in the field, standing waist-deep between ears of wheat and holding a stick that could be the handle of an agricultural tool; the photograph is entitled "Two acres

of wheat planted and harvested on the Battery Park landfill, Manhattan".

12 Donadieu. *Campagnes Urbaines*, cit. The original edition was published in 1998.

13 Michel Corajoud, "Comment je fais" (letter, Paris, May 2004) now at http://corajoudmichel.nerim.net/10-textes/01a-comment.htm

14 Samantha Hardingham, Kester Rattenbury, Bernard Tschumi, *Parc de la Villette. SuperCrit #4*, London: Routledge, 2011

15 Peter Eisenman, "Diagram: An Original Scene of Writing", in *Any*, no. 23, (1998), 27–29 in which Eisenman refers to Derrida's essay "Notes on the Freudian model of language" in *Writing and Difference*, London: Routledge, 1978. See also: Alexis Meier, *Peter Eisenman. Machine critique de l'architecture*, Gollion: Infolio, 2019

16 Jacques Lucan, *OMA Rem Koolhaas*, Milano: Electa, 2003. There is a further extensive bibliography on the project.

17 Luc Boltanski and Ève Chiapello *The New Spirit of Capitalism*, London: Verso Books, 2007 (first ed. 1999)

18 Max Weber, *The Protestant Ethic and the Spirit of Capitalism*, London: Penguin, 2002 (first ed. 1905)

19 Corajoud, *Le paysage, c'est l'endroit o. le ciel et la terre se touchent*, Actes sud.

20 Michel Foucault, *The Utopian Body*, radio lecture delivered in 1966. Published in *Sensorium*, Boston: MIT Press, 2006, 229–234, cit: 233

21 Corajoud, "Tutto è patrimonio", cit: 38

22 Bernardo Secchi, *La città del XX secolo*; Bari: Laterza, 2010: 56–57

23 See Chapter 1, note 9.

24 John Dewey, *Art as Experience*, Tarcherperigree, London: Penguin, 2005 (first ed. 1934)

25 Zheng Bo, *Pteridophilia 1*, 2016 Video (4k colour, sound) 17'; *Pteridophilia 2*, 2018, Video (4k colour, sound) 20'. See: Marco Scotini (ed.), *Zheng Bo. Weed Party III / Il partito delle erbacce*, Pteridophilia, Torino: PAV (4.11.2018–24.2.2019)

26 Jean-Luc Nancy, *Il corpo dell'arte*, Milano: Mimesis, 2014, a collection of five essays in Italian edited by Daniela Calabrò and Dario Giuliano

27 Baruch Spinoza, *Ethics*, London: Penguin Books, 1951, Part III Postulate I. Part II. Prop. XIII

28 Gabriele Pasqui, *La città, i saperi, le pratiche*, Roma: Donzelli, 2018

29 Gilles Deleuze, *Spinoza*, Paris: PUF, 1970, in Italian. The posthumous collection of the lessons held in Vincennes in 1980–81, edited by Aldo Pardi, *Lezioni su Spinoza (Cosa può un corpo? Lezioni su Spinoza*, Verona: Ombre Corte, 2007). Deleuze clarifies the position of the Dutch philosopher: being affected is a constitutive feature of the body and bodies are affects in specific circumstances. Nature and culture determine the possibility of being affected in various ways. Affect is the variation of the power of acting: the way in which the body increases its potential.

30 Spinoza, *Ethics*, cit. Part II prop. XIII Postulate IV

31 Anthony Vidler, *The Architectural Uncanny. Essays in the Modern Unhomely*, London: MIT Press, 1992

32 Johan Huizinga, *Homo ludens. A Study of the Play-Element in Culture*, London: Routledge, 1949: 7–12

33 Vidler, *The Architectural Uncanny. Essays in the Modern Unhomely*, cit.

34 Boltanski and Chiapello, *The New Spirit of Capitalism*, cit.

35 Huizinga was described as "incredibly awkward" by Delio Cantimori, one of the most accredited modernist historians of twentieth-century Italian historiography. Vittorio Foa called him "a Dutch cheese eater" in one of his letters from prison in the summer of 1938. Clearly, we cannot say that Huizinga's studies were welcomed enthusiastically in Italy in the late thirties (although they were to become internationally successful when *Homo Ludens* was published). At the time, his ideas were contained in the book *The crisis of civilisation*, translated into Italian in 1937. Reactions are cited in Michele Bonsarto's introduction to the new edition of this study entitled *Nelle ombre del domani*, Torino: Aragno, 2019

36 Vidler, *The Architectural Uncanny*, cit.

37 Spinoza, *Ethics*, cit. Part II, postulate IV

38 Cristina Bianchetti, *Il Novecento*

è davvero finito. Considerazioni sull'urbanistica, Roma: Donzelli, 2011

39 Chantal Mouffe provides a radical interpretation of the results of the work performed by Boltanski and Chiapello, re-interpreting it on the basis of the concept of hegemony and passive revolution. Chantal Mouffe, "Radical Politics as Counter-Hegemonic Intervention: the Role of Cultural Practices" in Mohsen Mostafavi (edited by), *Ethics of the Urban. The City and the Spaces of the Political*, Zürich: Müller, 2017: 209–231

40 Greg Lynn (ed.), *Archaeology of the Digital*, Berlin: CCA – Stenberg Press, 2013; Andrew Goodhouse (ed.), *When is the Digital in Architecture?*, Berlin: Sternberg, 2017

41 Giuliana Bruno, *Atlante delle emozioni*, Milano: Bruno Mondadori, 2002

42 Peter Sloterdijk, *Sphären I. Blasen*, Frankfurt/Main: Suhrkamp Verlag, 1998

43 Piter Bialobrezeski, *Heimat*, Berlin: Hatje Cantz Pub., 2005

44 Augustin Berque, *Écoumène. Introduction à l'ètude des milieux humains*, Paris: Belin, 2015: 52

45 That "feeling which he would like to call a sensation of eternity, a feeling as of something limitless, unbounded, something 'oceanic'." Freud talks about this in the introduction to *Civilisation and Its Discontents*, London: Penguin, 2002: 2. In 1929 Freud was 72 years old, the psychoanalytical movement was in shreds and Europe—the western world—was going through a very bad patch. In the opening lines of his last, bitter book, Freud recalls how his positions on religion had been criticised by a friend, Romain Rolland, who in reply to his *Future of Illusion* talks of a feeling that never left him and which had been expressed by other individuals. A "feeling of something limitless, unbounded – as it were 'oceanic'". Not a postulate of faith, even if it were a source of energy that he felt he could say was almost religious. An oceanic feeling. The idea of "we shall not fall out of this world". A feeling of indissoluble adhesion, of communion with the outside world. Freud answered by returning to the reasons and boundaries of the ego.

46 Vittorio Lingiardi, *Mindscapes. Psiche nel paesaggio*, Milano: Raffaello Cortina, 2017: 66

47 This is the English title of a play by Luigi Pirandello from 1917.

48 Everything experienced in uncertainty: "*qu'est-ce qu'un paysage? Assez vite, j'ai compris qu'on ne devait s'appliquer à cerner cette notion d'une façon trop précise*". Inexact notions, the advantage of imprecision: "*le paysage … ce qui rend difficile sa définition et cette difficulté est un*", Michel Corajoud, "L'Horizon, Interview pour la revue Face", (5 March 2004) at http://corajoudmichel.nerim.net/10-textes/01a-horizon.htm

THE LOSS OF THE BODY

*For there is no ghost, there is
never any becoming-spectre
of the spirit without at least
an appearance of flesh …
For there to be a ghost,
there must be a return to
the body, but to a body that
is more abstract than ever.*
Derrida, 1994[1]

Frankfurt 1929, Amsterdam 1931

How many ways are there to lose the body? It can be lost in form, structure, and measurement. There have been numerous attempts at standardisation in which the body remains the implicit premise, frozen in its repetitive, standardised movements. Reduced to a silhouette, weightless, unable to act if not automatically and predictably. Reduced to nothing, to a sign, a number, a stamp, a mugshot. The nineteenth century used judicial anthropometry as a tool. The twentieth century continued to seek to standardise the body in other ways. As long as we think in terms of numbers, measurements, and standards, we still think, like it or not, in terms of incorporeal substance.

Frankfurt 1929—the concept of the "minimum *modus vivendi*"[2] or "*Existenzminimum*".[3] In the field of architecture, 1929 is remembered for the repertoire of *Existenzminimum* plans presented in Frankfurt[4] by modernist architects concerned with rebuilding urban space from its foundations up; they designed images of a city in which myths were revived. Every move, every element, reflected a "strict discipline" and "moral rule".[5] Different from previous efforts, this project concerning inhabited space was to be imposed on disorderly practices; the new spaces shaped like shiny, perfectly functional machines. The story is far too famous for it to be repeated here. But I would just like to cite the definition by Giancarlo De Carlo regarding this issue: he writes that it involved proposing finite types to be implemented for uses corresponding to normalised groups of needs.[6] A concise and rather ungenerous definition.

At the CIAM in Frankfurt in 1929, the lack of collective proposals was accompanied by an "exasperated adherence to machinist-technology":[7] ten years earlier, Max Weber had already written that the exasperated adherence to technology was the expression of rationalisation and intellectualisation, and—above all,—of the disenchantment of the world.[8] There was exasperation not only with regard to building practices, but also concerning the internal functioning of inhabitable space: the smaller the space, the greater the need for more and better equipment. Thanks to a system of sliding walls and fold-away furniture, multiple actions could be performed in just a few square meters. The *Applecroft Home Experiment Station* in Greenlawn had been launched in 1913. It was undertaken by a real Schumpeterian innovator and, moreover, by a woman: Christine Frederick. She used chronometers and diagrams to study workflows and efficiency at a workstation. Putting aside the Victorian idea of how to manage and organise a family, Frederick decided to apply the same scientific principles that applied to a factory workplace to household chores.[9] The domestic appeal of Taylorism became a key focus of Christine Frederick's work; it modernised the private, family space, and by so doing decreased the time needed for household chores—tasks usually performed by women.

The topic tackled in Frankfurt was "the problem of the minimum dwelling", as cited in the opening of Water Gropius' presentation to the congress.[10] During this season of extensive building programmes,[11] it was the concept of dwelling itself that was radically redefined based on political tensions, trust in scientific methods, rationalisation, and Taylorisation. It has been noted that, during the season of early functionalism,[12] not only were incredible quantitative bases developed for empirical studies on the city, dwelling, and individuals, but efforts were made to legitimise positions believed to be morally right. The fairytale of the world was beginning all over again and, like all fairytales, it brought with it apocalyptic messages, utopian ambitions, and the values of a transparent moralism,[13] transferred primarily into the scientific-quantitative discourse. Architects find this quite appealing.

The plans for the minimum dwelling were redesigned on the same scale as previously, compared with one another, and deconstructed. Movement and life were possible in these plans, but bodies were not. The plans contained rights, ideology. Complex cultural and organisational operations. The sought-after "coincidence of political and intellectual authority" cited by Manfredo Tafuri in *Progetto e Utopia*.[14] All of these are present, but bodies are not. When you think about it, Tafuri's metaphor of the assembly line alludes to this decoupling.[15] It's a metaphor that should not only be considered in a machinist, organisational sense, but as a violent abstraction that turns bodies into a workforce.

1931 Amsterdam—the concept of "minimum effort",[16] the "acceptable vital minimum";[17] the "minimum real demand to be satisfied by the country's resources".[18] Between the late twenties and the early thirties, the obsession for the minimum resurfaces constantly. This is not surprising, as those were the years that followed on the heels of the Great Depression. One of the most important international conferences on the dissemination of scientific management methods was held in Amsterdam in 1931. This was when the concept of *planism* was developed and bounced backwards and forwards between the United States and Europe.[19] It hinged, once again, on the problem of the minimum. The World Social Economic Planning conference[20] was the world stage for the Taylor Society, but also for the ideas of Henry Ford and Thorstein Veblen. Or, more precisely, for the perspective of engineers on the Depression. In the United States, this view was conveyed by *The New Republic*, the liberal magazine to which John Dewey was a regular contributor. It's worth mentioning that, with Cor van Eesteren's plan, Amsterdam taught European urbanism a crucial lesson during that period; it was during the halcyon days of the plan, in both the field of economics and in terms of urban projects. Another very evident occurrence at that time was the decoupling of the idea of the plan itself (as a tool to organise orderly, comprehensive development) and the organisation of productive forces—a discordant, unrestrainable organisation lacking in appeasing solutions.[21] The authority of the plan shattered against the dynamic imbalances of capitalism. At the same time, the Amsterdam congress launched the season of managerial planning. This was a season marked by the dissemination of a scientific viewpoint, of trust in method and technique; of the failure not only to tolerate but also to simply see the confused constellation of practices on which, de facto, all plans depend. The presentations in Amsterdam were very clear:

the way work is planned in a factory can also be the way to "conduct business in the world".[22] A little like Christine Frederick's experiments in the kitchen. A social group (engineers, technicians), considering themselves to be hegemonic, believed they were the only ones who knew "what is technically and objectively best for the community".[23] And that it was necessary to adjust things on a larger scale. American Taylorism clearly posed the problem of the relationship between technical reason and political reason.[24]

The words of the American engineers clearly indicate the values of individualism, self-esteem, intuition, and responsibility.[25] These values represent a broad vision that built its own techniques: those of the census, map, statistics, *tableaux*, catalogue, list, and diagram. When everything is stripped back to its minimum, techniques are omnivores; they self-produce, and suffer no limitation.

Those were the years when Frederick W. Taylor was credited with the best intentions: those of increased wellbeing, harmonious industrial relations, fair profits, high salaries, and low prices.[26] Taylorism was ambitious: its objective was to be exported everywhere, to involve everyone, to stimulate and be coupled with nascent planning. In other words, to reintroduce good management in places where *laissez faire* had led to disorder and diseconomies. Its principles aimed to reduce social complexity and conflicts within the framework of process management, coupled with a depersonalised chain of command. So if things didn't work, it was no longer a question of exploitation, dominance, and conflict, but one of bad management.[27]

A Better World

There were multiple approaches at the Amsterdam congress: the European approach focused intently on trying to find a way to apply the "engineer's viewpoint" on social issues to the old continent,[28] while the American Fordist approach adhered to the slogan "Mass Production Makes a Better World".[29] An extraordinary slogan, containing and expressing the utopian, referring to a world in which there would be more merchandise, available to all, and at affordable prices. And so, in turn, the merchandise would also produce consumers. A "better world" that may make us either smile or shiver, but which was undoubtedly the sign of a confidently and obstinately pursued modernisation. Like many utopias, this one left behind many remnants; in the physical space of our cities, in our trust in protocols, in technological answers to complex problems, and in what was ultimately reduced responsibility over and for processes.[30] What is a smart city if not the contemporary rewriting of these principles? Another "better world". Every age probably has one. But oh, how similar the Fordist world and our smart world look! They are both better worlds because they can manage big numbers.[31] Worlds that profess themselves to be irremediably democratic. Both striving to provide new solutions to old problems. Both very urban. The former envisages a Ford T car—possibly black—for everyone. The latter imagines that the car can drive itself, leaving behind it a web of minute, precious pieces of information. The former works with steel, asphalt, and concrete. The latter with lithium and silicon. Both are obsessed with time, measurement, data, technologies, and control. Both contemplate an almost infantile idea of innovation.

We should seriously ask ourselves whether criticising the infantile vagueness of this enthusiasm for the smart city expresses the diffidence that has always accompanied the critique of technology and progress. We know that culture, especially Italian culture, has extensively exploited the right to doubt progress. Just read Pasolini's *Lutheran Letters* on this issue. Is that why it's so difficult to believe in the beautiful fairytale of the smart city? In its virtuous proclaimed ability to accelerate change? In the happy mix between technology and business? In the promise of its skies, blue once again thanks to the fact that we have solved our energy and waste disposal problems? Perhaps we need to overcome our diffidence. We need Christine Frederick's courage. But also, undoubtedly, her intelligence.

Incorporeity / Dematerialisation

Frankfurt 1929; Amsterdam 1931. Everything is based on measurement. Measurement as a revolutionary act, as a definitive reduction of the weight of social values to a parameter. Something cold, abstract, neutral: the promise of a precise, objective, and eternally shareable description of reality; the ability to summarise in a few characters a disorderly variety and quantity of elements; the ability to control confusion; the ability to align reality to itself, to construct reality.[32]

In measurement, the body evaporates. It becomes incorporeal. It loses posture, gait, gesture, mimicry, and vocal timbre. Loses substance. It becomes a weightless body that doesn't touch the ground. A presence reduced to a "spectre without at least an appearance of flesh", as per Derrida's words cited at the beginning of this chapter.[33] Today we would say that it plays a lesser role in the informative infrastructures that produce numbers in the form of tables, graphs, and digital data. Yesterday we would have said the same of its role in cybernetics and, earlier still, in Alexander Klein's big comparative tables. But one could go back even further to Alphonse Bertillon's descriptions of a dissected body.[34] In all these cases, the body evaporates into quantities, measurements, algorithms, and actions repeated ad infinitum in modern kitchens. Measurement and standardisation have not only created the extraordinary quantitative bases for empirical studies on the city, dwelling, and individuals. They have also marked the zero point of the body as a link between space and the urban project.

Loss of the body involves its multiplication into a tendentially unlimited, simplified series of numbers or fragments. Merleau-Ponty writes that "the spoken word is significant not only through the medium of individual words, but also through that of accent, intonation, gesture and facial expression".[35] So, too, is loss of the body loss of all this. It is loss of substance: accent, intonation, gesture, and facial expression. In the representation of the urban project and architecture, the body is often multiplied in small, weightless symbols, little figures in drawings, once stylised, now more realistic in order to reflect a dogmatic variation: cyclist, child, older person, a rainbow family. Little figures separated by space even when (especially when) they have been put there to suggest the public nature of a place. This form of incorporeity turns the body into a transit channel that is too weak, too predefined, that is conventional and mute: an *a priori* that doesn't provide a hold, when in truth our body has a form, density, outline, and weight. It occupies a place. Having a body "is … to be intervolved in a definite environment, to identify oneself with certain projects and be continually committed to them", and "we must therefore avoid saying that our body is in space, or in time. It inhabits space and time".[36] We are united and confused with, and committed to, a specific, definite environment. In Sartre's words, "being there is precisely the body".[37] We live in space with the encumbrance of our bodies. This exposes us, but at the same time empowers action. Action cannot be reduced to a sign. It cannot be suggested, implied, suspended in measurements concerning the body. All phenomenology is a discourse on this state of being engaged in the world: of being touched, invested, enlightened by the world insofar as we are bodies. Insofar as we are caught up in specific circumstances.

Incorporeity is therefore the body denying its presence. It narrates individuals who—in measurements, in rights, in economic rationalities,—are bodiless. They are Enzensberger's "statistical ghosts".[38] Individuals with only one role: salaried workers, consumers, insurance contractors, investors, stockholders, entrepreneurs, or savers. Or, equally, the sick, the poor, the crazy, or refugees. It is the functionalist theatre and its puppets to which the concept of the abstract rationality of the economy has contributed. The same goes for the law, with another no-less-powerful abstraction: the owner-individual at the heart of modern constitutionalism.[39] And the same can be said again for medicine.

The heretical tradition of social and economic philosophy brings into play interests and passions, but moves in the direction opposite to that of functionalist, economic, juridical and medical orthodoxy. This tradition was followed by anthropologists such as Marcel Mauss[40] and Marshall Sahlins,[41] as well as atypical sociologists such as Georg Simmel and Gabriel Tarde.[42] It was also followed by Karl Polanyi, with the copresence of pre-capitalist and advanced economic relations,[43] and obviously by Albert Hirschman, the author of *The Passions and the Interests*:[44] the first chapter of his book is entitled "How the Interests were called upon to counteract the Passions". In it, the individual appears with all his bridled, repressed emotions and is turned into a counterweight to action.

Incorporeity recalls the parallel process of the derealisation of things and, we can easily add, of spaces reduced to neutral, smooth surfaces that are also bereft of "accent, intonation, gesture, and facial expression".[45] Many authors would eventually revive the topic. One of these was Roberto Esposito, who dedicated a small but important book to two contrary and complementary processes: the *depersonalisation* of individuals and the *derealisation* of things.[46] The book focuses on the crux of the matter: Esposito writes that the genealogy of the concept of the individual is the result of progressive abstraction which, in the end, clearly uncouples it from the body.[47]

Losing the Body

How many ways are there to lose the body? It can be lost in form, structure, and measurement. Undoubtedly in these ways; but there are also many other ways. In positions that ignore the fact that the body exists in an increasingly emphasised dislocation between natural and technological traits; between a "conform" condition and one which tends to be constantly evolving; between sexuality and identity; between old and new types of families as the result of new possible conceptions and filiations. The body is lost in every compression of this abundant, growing variety. In every collective imagery that perhaps enhances the body by emptying it. In the dislocations that project it far away, in virtual reconstructions. The body is lost when cultivating a sense of time similar to a fantasy of eternity that denies the idea of death as the end of a journey. Freud believed that the death drive is not countered by the life instinct: everyone "wishes to die only in their own fashion", and tries to implement this in a complex and tortuous manner.[48] Finally, the body is lost when celebrating the transparent or "transparency" society, a term used by Byung-Chul Han in the title of his recent book.[49] The *transparency society* is a contemporary mythography: in other words, the opposite of everything written by and about Bentham and Foucault—but also (and again in contrast to) Popper's open society and all those who cite it in order to talk about the city (most recently Richard Sennett, in the magazine *Lotus*).[50]

Are not transparency, aperture, and freedom respectable and desirable political and urban ideals as well as ways to achieve incorporeity? Does not the transparent state of the subject and space, unveiled, exposed, and afforded to forms of control, contribute to incorporeity and dematerialisation? How will the urban project, always so attentive towards the stratified physical and material nature of places, tackle the bodily loss of space and those who live in it?

Notes

1   Jacques Derrida, *Specters of Marx. The State of the Debt, the Work of Mourning and the New International*, London: Routledge, 1994: 157
2   Walter Gropius, "I presupposti sociologici per l'alloggio minimo", in Carlo Aymonino (ed.), *L'abitazione razionale. Atti dei congressi C.I.A.M. 1929–1930*, Venezia: Marsilio, 1971: 102–112
3   Alexander Klein, "Ricerca sulla progettazione razionale delle piante di alloggi a superficie minima" in Matilde Baffa Rivolta and Augusto Rossari (eds.), *Alexander Klein. Lo studio delle piante e la progettazione degli spazi negli alloggi minimi. Scritti e progetti dal 1906 al 1957*, Milano: Mazzotta, 1975: 115–128
4   The 29th and 30th CIAM Congresses, held in Frankfurt and Brussels respectively. The Italian translation of the proceedings of these two important CIAM congresses were published in the book *L'abitazione razionale. Atti dei congressi C.I.A.M. 1929–1930* by Carlo Aymonino cit. A year before Frankfurt, in 1928, Klein published a famous comparative assessment method for apartment plans (Alexander Klein, "Grundrissbildung und Raumgestaltung von Kleinwohnungen und neue Auswertungsmethoden" in *Zentralblatt der Bauverwaltung*, Berlin, 1928, no. 33 and 34. Italian translation in Baffa Rivolta and Rossari, *Alexander Klein. Lo studio delle piante e la progettazione degli spazi negli alloggi minimi. Scritti e progetti dal 1906 al 1957*, cit: 77 et foll.). It involved a certain number of spacious housing types that were investigated using empirical and logical assessments. Klein was seeking a method of scientific

assessment, comparison, and design (an instrument that many manuals were later to propose). In his study, the architectural object is diluted into three dimensions. The first of these is *Assessment*, using questionnaires, classifications, and lists; this is considered a primarily technical issue. The concern was that judgement is subjective, empathic, and difficult to sustain. Strict correction coefficients are employed to offset this danger. Second is *Comparison*: a simpler issue that involved using the same scale for the whole design to enable comparison of the solutions in plan. Thirdly, *Design* is a deductive process comparing all the features of the plan with the layout of the pathways, the arrangement of the areas earmarked for routes, and the concentration of surfaces free from any furnishings (Ivi: 35 and 36). We could call it the quantification of design.

5   Giorgio Grassi, "Das Neue Frankfurt e l'architettura della nuova Francoforte" in Id., ed. *Das Neue Frankfurt 1926–1931*, Bari: Dedalo, 1975: 9

6   Words on the back cover of the Italian edition of the book by John Habraken, *Supports: an alternative to mass housing*, London: The Architectural Press, 1972. See below in chapter 5.

7   Matilde Baffa, "Alexander Klein e il problema della casa nella Germania di Weimar". Introduction to *Alexander Klein. Lo studio delle piante e la progettazione degli spazi negli alloggi minimi. Scritti e progetti dal 1906 al 1957*, 7–18, cit.: 17

8   Max Weber, *Science as Vocation*, in David Owen and Tracy Strong (eds.), *The Vocation Lectures*, Illinois: Hackett Books, 2004 (first ed. 1919)

9   Frederick addressed the middle classes and wrote in the *Ladies' Home Journal*. She published *The New Housekeeping* (1913). She was not the only one to do so: Georgie Child published the book *The Efficient Kitchen* (1914) and, during that period, Martha and Robert Bruère published *Increasing Home Efficiency* (1912). But Frederick was the one who focused most on Taylorism to "scientifically" innovate domestic labour and household spaces. The

famous *Frankfurter Küche* by Margarete Schütte-Lihotzky was not published till 1926. See: Catherine Clarisse, *Cuisine, recettes d'architecture*, Besançon: Les Editeurs de l'Imprimeur, 2004; and more recently, Imma Forino, *La cucina. Storia culturale di un luogo domestic*, Torino: Einaudi, 2019. Regarding Frederick's innovative and entrepreneurial spirit, see also https://www.ediblelongisland.com/2014/03/17/christine-frederick-kitchen-innovator-efficiency/

10 Walter Gropius "The problem of the minimum dwelling is to establish the elementary minimum of space, air, light and heat necessary to men to develop their own vital functions without restrictions due to the lodging, in other words a minimum modus vivendi, instead of a *modus non moriendi*". In "*Sociological Premises for the Minimum Dwelling*", in Augusto Rossari, "Gli studi di Alexander Klein e il movimento razionalista", in *Alexander Klein. Lo studio delle piante e la progettazione degli spazi negli alloggi minimi. Scritti e progetti dal 1906 al 1957*, 31–41, cit: 37. It represents a concept of lodging defined as "anabolic"; living space catalyses and preserves the energy of its inhabitants and enables its assimilation. On second thoughts, the opposite is also true: living space can express dissipation—catabolism, if we wish to maintain the same metaphor. It is a privileged place of intimacy, rest, and the refuelling of manpower. A place of loss of energy, degradation, and dispersion (which nevertheless sparks the release of excess energy). These points can be found in Engels (*The Condition of the Working Class in England*, London: Penguin, 1987) and Hannes Meyer, "The architecture of capitalist housing in the post-war period, 1919–1934", translation of the original version in the Meyer archive, cited in Hannes Meyer *Architettura o rivoluzione. Scritti 1921–1942*, Francesco Dal Co (ed.), Padova: Marsilio, 1969: 162–170

11 Barbara Miller Lane, *Architecture and Politics in Germany 1918–1945*, Cambridge: Harvard University Press, 1968. Cited also by Tafuri, *Progetto e*

Utopia, Bari: Laterza, 1973–2007, note 69, p. 106

12 Kees Somer, "A clear message to the Outside World. Drawing Conclusions and Publishing the Results of CIAM 4" in Evelien van Es, Gregor Harbusch, Bruno Maurer, Muriel Pérez, Kees Somer, Daniel Weiss (eds.), *Atlas of the Functional City. CIAM 4 and Comparative Urban Analysis*, Bussum: THOTH Publishers Verlag, 2014: 72–82

13 Literally: making *home* the field of exercise for demonstrations inspired by the logic of value. Conscious, or perhaps not, that the conversion of living space into values makes the commensurable incommensurable. Carl Schmitt, *The Tyranny of Values*, Washington: Plutarch Press, 1996

14 Tafuri, *Progetto e Utopia*, cit. Tafuri attributes the task of mediating between structure and superstructure to the coincidence of political and intellectual authority. It's useful to cite the passage on pp. 105–106: "The utopism of Middle-European architecture culture between the twenties and thirties consists of the fiduciary relationship between leftist intellectuals, advanced sectors of 'democratic capitalism' (e.g., Rathenau), and democratic administrations. In this framework, while sectorial solutions tend to appear as highly generalised models – state policies, expropriations, technological experiments, formal elaboration of the Siedlung type – they reveal their limited efficiency when tested with facts."

15 Ivi: what is reproduced in those experiences, in the city, is "the disaggregated form of the paleotechnic assembly line. The city remains an aggregate of parts, functionally united at a minimum level; and even within each individual 'piece' – the working-class neighbourhood – the unification of methods quickly reveals itself to be an aleatory tool". Ivi: 106–107

16 De Man, cited in Alfredo Salsano, *Ingegneri e politici. Dalla razionalizzazione alla "rivoluzione manageriale"*, Torino: Einaudi, 1987: 30

17 Presentation by Lorwin at the *World Social Economic Planning Congress,*

cited in A. Salsano, *Ingegneri e politici. Dalla razionalizzazione alla "rivoluzione manageriale"*, cit: 17

18 Ibidem

19 For American exponents of social-progressive planning who express their ideas on this issue, see, for example, Lewis Levine Lorwin: an outline in Salsano, *Ingegneri e politici. Dalla razionalizzazione alla "rivoluzione manageriale"*, cit: 15

20 Mary L. Fleddérus (International Industrial Relations Institute – I.R.I.), *World Social Economic Planning; the necessity for planned adjustment of productive capacity and standards of living. Material contributed to the World Social Economic Congress, Amsterdam, August, 1931*, The Hague, International Industrial Relations Institute, Holland, N.Y. (I.R.I.), 1932

21 Manfredo Tafuri, "Per una critica dell'ideologia architettonica", *Contropiano*, no. 1, (1969), 31–79

22 Salsano, *Ingegneri e politici. Dalla razionalizzazione alla "rivoluzione manageriale"*, cit: 10.

23 Lorwin in Salsano, *Ingegneri e politici. Dalla razionalizzazione alla "rivoluzione manageriale"*, cit.: 18

24 This is the key issue in the book by Salsano, who wished to demonstrate that, even if it is true that "Taylorised" industries prospered in Keynesian policies and then went downhill together, it is also true that the two strategies (those of the engineers and the politicians in the title) remain fundamentally separate, despite echoes in European socialism. This topic was also tackled by Carlo Olmo in *Architecture and 20th Century. Rights Conflicts Values*, Trento: List, 2013

25 In the report by Perenson, cited in Salsano, *Ingegneri e politici. Dalla razionalizzazione alla "rivoluzione manageriale"*, cit.: 12

26 Person, cit. on p. 170 in Salsano, *Ingegneri e politici. Dalla razionalizzazione alla "rivoluzione manageriale"*, cit.: 12

27 Management is a key issue. It chiefly exploits cooperation (social problems become problems of cooperation, i.e., of

human relations). And planning is the framework of cooperation. However, we must undoubtedly acknowledge that these postulates lasted longer than those of Taylorism which, as we all know, prospered in Keynesian policies and then both went downhill together.

28 De Man, to whom Salsano dedicated ample space. Salsano, *Ingegneri e politici. Dalla razionalizzazione alla "rivoluzione manageriale"*, cit.: 24 et foll.

29 Edward A. Filene cited in Salsano, *Ingegneri e politici. Dalla razionalizzazione alla "rivoluzione manageriale"*, cit.: 22

30 Carlo Olmo, "Introductory Lecture", *Seminar Cycle FULL*, 11 June 2018, Polytechnic of Turin.

31 So much has been said about our current governance using numbers. Here I shall only cite the introduction by Ota de Leonardis and Federico Neresini, "Il potere dei grandi numeri" in the monographic issue of *RSI* no. 3–4 (2015), 371–378

32 This belief was present throughout those years, but also exists now. In the broad debate that currently juxtaposes emancipatory potentials and the coercive power of quantifications, critical orientations, and deconstructions of quantitative data, we are very distant from the season of planism: referring to it would be considered a provocation. Besides, everything has changed: the potential of surplus quantitative informative bases, management technologies and the role they play in knowledge, the metamorphoses of contemporary capitalism, and forms of knowledge as a matrix of the production of value. But in my opinion, the appeal of quantification at least appears to possess the same tones and still survives the corruption of the principles of urban design, at least that of the principle that promised stability, hierarchy, and generalised and modular applications for mass usefulness and universal aesthetics. This is the enigma of contemporary quantification, which still exists, although its political background has disappeared—unlike what happened in the twenties.

33 Jacques Derrida, *Specters of Marx: The State of the Debt, the Work of Mourning and the New International*, translated by Peggy Kamuf, London: Routledge, 1994: 157

34 Alphonse Bertillon was the director of the identification bureau of the Paris Prefecture in the early 1880s. When faced with serious social problems during the period of industrialisation, mass movement, impoverishment, and the exponential growth of urban density, Bertillon proposed an anthropomorphic identification system combining the anthropomorphic descriptive analysis of the individual (measurements of the body, limbs, facial features, eye colour, etc.), a photograph based on pre-established rules (front and profile), classification of the identification cards, and their conservation based on certain rules. The archives of the prefecture were important places during the construction of nineteenth- and twentieth-century nationalisms.

35 Maurice Merleau-Ponty, *Phenomenology of Perception*, London: Routledge, 2002: 174

36 Ivi: 94 and 161

37 Jean-Paul Sartre, *Being and Nothingness: an Essay on Phenomenological Ontology*, New York: Philosophical Library, 1992: 461. He poses a relational perspective with regard to this issue: to be there is also "the shock of the encounter with the Other"; "a revelation … of my body outside as an in-itself for the Other". *Ibidem.*

38 Magnus Enzensberger, *Panopticon: Twenty Ten-Minute Essays*, London – New York: Seagull Books, 2018; translation from the Italian edition, *Panopticon. Venti saggi da leggere in dieci minuti*, Torino: Einaudi, 2019: 6

39 Property built as sovereignty over things creates the juridical person. In his *Introduzione al Novecento giuridico*, Paolo Grossi writes about the individual of modern civil law as a virtual, abstract person: "he is the citizen of the old eighteenth-century charters of rights, a citizen identical to every other", an "artificial" individual, "marked by abstractness". Paolo Grossi, *Introduzione*

al Novecento giuridico, Bari: Laterza, 2012: 21 and 25

40 Marcel Mauss, *The Gift: The Form and Reason for Exchanges in Archaic Societies,* London: Routledge, 2002

41 Marshall Sahlins, *Culture and Pratical Reasons*, Chicago: University of Chicago, 1976

42 Tarde was a sociologist, criminologist, and philosopher. His studies on the *The Laws of Imitation*, (New York: Henry Holt and Company, 1903) revive an extremely multifaceted idea of the individual.

43 Karl Polanyi, *The Great Transformation*, Boston: Beacon Press, 1944; Karl Polanyi and others (eds.), *Trade and Market in the Early Empires: Economies in History and Theory*, Detroit: The Free Press, 1957

44 Albert O. Hirschman, *The Passions and the Interests. Political Arguments for Capitalism before its Triumph*, New Jersey: Princeton University Press, 1977

45 Merleau-Ponty, *Phenomenology of Perception*, cit.: 174

46 Roberto Esposito, *Le parole e le cose*, Torino: Einaudi, 2014: XII

47 The indomitable, albeit minority antagonist of this nihilistic outcome is present in a traditional idea Esposito attributes to Spinoza, one which, by way of Vico, is passed to Nietzsche and the French phenomenology of Merleau-Ponty, Sartre, and all those who oppose the irreversible severing of the soul from the body, of a person from things.

48 Sigmund Freud, *Beyond the Pleasure Principle*, New York: Liveright Publishing Corporation, 1961

49 Byung-Chul Han, *The Transparency Society*, USA: Stanford University Press, 2015

50 Richard Sennett, "La città aperta/The Open City" in Lotus, no. 168, (2019), 117–129

THE BODY THAT OFFERS ITSELF AS ENTERTAINMENT

*The body is the being-exposed
of the being.*
Nancy, 2014[1]

The New American City

The interior is a classic subject in architecture. Normally discussed in relation to the architectural artefact or to inhabited spaces, the interior has not ventured far into the field of urban planning. Charles Rice is one of the few who have tackled the urban dimension of the interior. In his book *Interior Urbanism,* he repositions the subject within the American experience of the sixties and seventies.[2] Rice's approach is typological, applied to a specific kind of interior: the lobby of big tertiary complexes, particularly those designed by John Portman & Associates in the two final decades of the Golden Age. His theory is that the lobbies of big urban buildings best represent the new consumer society of the sixties. This theory differs little from the traditional approach, which considers interiors as microcosms typical of the period during which administrative, judicial, educational, cultural, and consumer buildings were constructed in the modern city. The idea of the interior is established as the materialisation of the public domain. Or, rather, as the idea of a re-location of public life into big, built spaces: a process of "interiorisation of the public" that continued in the contemporary city as a result of more sophisticated functional and climatic systems.[3] In this chapter I would like to propose a different concept of the urban interior, starting with Rice's study.

Interior Urbanism opens with a splendid, grey-toned photograph of the *Renaissance Centre* in Detroit, which was designed by John Portman in 1977.

The photo by Timothy Hursley was taken a year after the sprawling complex, which was later to become the headquarters of General Motors, was built. The image was also published in the catalogue of the exhibition "Transformation in Modern Architecture" organised by MoMA in 1979. The photo has great visual force: a central, eye-level perspective culminating in the three imposing towers of the complex, its contours almost dematerialised by fog and smoke. In the foreground, a rail track with two parallel carriages that create two continuous wings converging on the towers; in the middle, three barely discernable figures with their backs to the onlooker. It's winter, there's fog, the men are wearing hats and heavy clothing and are carrying small suitcases, indicating that they belong to the middle class. Instant comparisons springs to mind: the Tower of Babel in *Metropolis* or the Tyrell Corporation in *Blade Runner*. The image of a future that has already arrived.

Rice's theory is that the lobbies of these big modernist complexes, with their multilevel, interconnected corridors, their small, unusual lounges for short "pit stops" halfway up the building, and their big, empty centres, are *Urban Interiors* that narrate modernisation better than anything else. Atlanta was the *New American City*, catalysed in the polished marble of its big tertiary and commercial complexes designed for a different society.

Rice explores the subject in several directions; he recalls the principles of a design process meticulously focused on comfort and climate control, brilliantly portrayed by the many hanging gardens.[4] He outlines the lively debates between unorthodox anthropologists such as Edward T. Hall[5] and academic sociologists like Robert Gutman and Herbert Gans,[6] reciprocally engaged in a discussion of the role of spatial proximity and the ways it generates behaviours. Human ecology, sociology, and design theory merge in these incredible suspended hollow spaces in real estate towers.

Urban Interiors

Rice's beautiful images do not contain bodies or traces of actions. They depict pure space, designed for functional, scenographic, and theatrical reasons. And, clearly, economic reasons. The photographs show the excavated interiors of solid masses. Rice considers the design of these hollow spaces as a specific way of conceiving and building the city. However, an essential dimension is lacking, and this absence enables the introduction of a diverse conceptualisation of what is meant by *Urban Interiors*, starting with the opening phrase by Nancy above: "the body is the being-exposed of the being".[7] *Urban Interiors* are urban spaces in which the body exposes, protects, and offers itself. It shows off an intimate and generally hidden part of itself. They are spaces experienced as though they are interiors, but in a very different manner to Rice's big lobbies (which, even today, are crowded places in cities—not just in America). Lobbies that are not necessarily suspended; that are often on the ground, with thresholds, passages, and openings that simultaneously give the impression of an embracing and yet absolutely free space. Interiors that have nothing to do with the house. These interiors are lighter. And they dissolve easily.

In recent years I have investigated interiors in Turin, both in my studies and while teaching:[8] interiors in public places, in the compact pattern of the city, in industrial areas and urban fringes. I have hunted down this specific form of space that makes urban compactness lighter and more mobile. *Urban Interiors* are not open to everyone, although they are not restricted in any way. They are generated by the density or uniqueness of the relations and practices of those who use them, by displays, attractions, repulsions, impulses, by holding on, by abandonment, possession, and dispossession. They are spaces of self-displacement, of the "dispossession" of one's own intimacy.[9] *Urban Interiors* are elastic spaces; they are deformed by time, either expanding or contracting. They are located in the space of the city, either inside or outside its buildings; they hook onto big infrastructures, civil and monumental buildings, like parasites; they insinuate themselves into more modest urban patterns according to logics that are not easy to trace. They are subject to seesaws of control and abandonment. They are everywhere: in urban fringes and old city centres. They are spaces that are chiefly used temporarily.

One could say, provocatively, that they are "voids" filled with relationships: cracks in a significant chain of uses of urban space that emphasise the latter's foreign, alienated nature:[10] spaces that are "foreign although they are central"; ones that are unknown, but which we feel are familiar. Their void is what contains relationships, bodies, and feelings of agitation. This is what space is. Space *that contains*. A meaningful gash that pierces reality, creating the possibility of establishing relations. Studying these spaces means introducing a different reasoning, one which space reveals the body engulfed in a scrimmage with other bodies. It narrates the bond of what is between the bodies. And what is between the bodies is not an ideal space, but a space either filled with or emptied of bodies.

We inhabit the city in our own agitations, desires, anxieties, actions, and obsessions. The material, carnal relationship with space is created by the body and by our senses. Senses are not doors we can open or close. The crucial topic raised by *Urban Interiors* involves the way in which the world enters the body through our senses.[11] I use the categories of *intimité* and *extimité* to tackle the issue of the relationship between space and the body; they help not only to arrange the weave of the *interiors*, starting with the relationships between bodies, but, at the same time, to completely rethink the urban.[12]

"My body's depth of being is for me the perpetual 'outside' of my most intimate 'inside'".[13] *Urban Interiors* convey the emergence of that "more intimate inside": an externality at the heart of the individual. In seminar no. VII, Lacan introduces the term *extimité*:[14] a one-word neologism used to highlight the density between exteriority and interiority; to indicate the movement that encourages the revelation of a part of our private physical and psychic life. A voluntary dispossession of a part of us. This device allows a relational interpretation of *Urban Interiors*, always balanced between a hypothetical inside and a just-as-hypothetical outside—between closure and display.

Inside. *Urban Interiors* are a bubble, a clearing, a shelter, where in isolation we can collect ourselves within an inward-looking dimension, a dimension where we wish to hide what we consider personal, be it affective or emotional. Hollow areas, interiors; at the antipodes of the meaning of the modern concept of public space. They are the spaces where we are alone in the midst of others, in an environment that remains open, permeable, and plural—and in its own way, crowded. Inside is where we escape others; a place of suspended time in which we can exist without interacting or speaking, far from the eyes of others—far from indiscrete, intrusive, Bentham-like eyes. Far from the supervision and action of what is around us. The right to remain hidden, to remain silent, is what asserts the person vis-à-vis the Other, removing the individual from the totalitarian power of the Other.

Outside. *Urban Interiors* are spaces in which we exhibit our inner world, creating exchanges with other individuals believed to have similar sensitivities, affinities, and desires. Spaces for coming out of oneself. For using one's self to create entertainment. For letting oneself go in the context of a relationship with others in which we lightly brush pass one another without holding on. Outside is where we display our own self, where we build ties with people we think share our values. A complex movement with the body at its centre. A body that reveals itself, exhibits passions and desires, at the same time is forced to deal with the needs and rules of coexistence. It is the demand for the right to warm relations in public space. In both cases there is a link with power and a specifically public dimension reiterating its relational and passionate nature.

The City Viewed Close Up

My first consideration is that this train of thought focuses closely on the city—very closely, from the viewpoint of bodies and their relationships. And that this is an inappropriate interpretation of the big agglomerations, metropolises, and vast continental territories that continuously emerge in our contemporary geographical and urban planning debate and, by so doing, orient and develop it. Almost as if it were a univocal direction. Pier Luigi Nicolin wrote: "Looking closely is not a narrow focus".[15] Perhaps this phrase is consolatory, but it is exactly what I believe regarding *Urban Interiors*, as well as regarding the plurality of bodies and their will either to be alone in the midst of others or to display themselves. Looking closely is not a narrow focus—even if the body undoubtedly "pulls downwards", drawing closer to the specific characteristics of the place, the action, and the sensations of those bodies. To angular spaces in which to either hide or display ourselves. The body pulls the idea of the public "downwards". The public is clothed by these spaces, albeit unwillingly; the body acts as a counterthrust, conjuring up spaciousness and horizontality.

The second consideration, linked to the first, is that a discussion about *Urban Interiors* and their relational ecology[16] requires an effort to suspend other imaginaries that we continue to use to reflect on the city and its design. It involves, for example, a distancing from the sharp delimitations of limits, margins, and figures in urbanism.[17] Delimitations that separate: areas in which real-estate pressure is applied differently; groups of more or less prestigious schools; areas of good or bad hospitals; areas in which police operations are performed more or less frequently; digital or technological networks; heavy infrastructures, factory walls, fences around gated communities, reclusion buildings, Roma camps, police barracks, etc. Demarcation lines, either drawn or perceived, are precisely where the phenomena tend to end or be reversed. They are perceived as sharp demarcations, easily recognised either by those who live in cities, even for a few months or weeks, or by visitors, as demarcations that have their own energy flows, inducing or dissuading behaviours. *Urban Interiors* can also be considered as frequency deviations in the energy of these demarcations. If we were to indicate them on a map, they would be a doodle; a more or less busy doodle, a more or less rambling doodle, breaking the continuity of these lines. They are complex spaces made complex by what happens within them. Compactness can be pierced or cracked and shamelessly reveal what is hidden inside. The linearity of borders and boundaries is broken and becomes complicated. Tensions are sparked. Touch, light, shadow, access, and shelter conditions are important, but not enough.

Finally, a discussion about *Urban Interiors* involves dealing with porosity and its meaning as defined by Benjamin, especially when he unquestioningly accepts the invitation to look for new, unexpected social configurations in courtyards, under arches, and in stairwells,[18] as well as when he looks at the city as if it were stone, full of hollows, voids, holes, and cracks: "the city has a rocky appearance". Porosity is a metaphor discussed in text after text, starting with the poetic and redundant essay about Naples by Walter Benjamin and the charming Asja Lācis. It is an essay that captures the intimacy of a city deeply loved by Benjamin for its Oedipal warmth, but deteriorated by modernity; a place where people exit rather than enter houses. One with a porosity not only of space, but of private and festive life, of its rhythms and schedules. Of civilian and religious practices. An intellectual circle—Benjamin, Ernst Bloch, and Theodor W. Adorno—celebrate Naples and an entire season.[19] The metaphor of porosity is constantly repeated. Countless lessons on urbanism have focused on Giambattista Nolli's 1748 map of Rome in which buildings are used as transit spaces, passages, and openings; a mysterious, fairytale urban pattern resulting from its hidden apertures and contiguities. The metaphor of porosity became particularly successful more recently: Ash Amin and Nigel Thrift wanted to establish what they call the "new urbanism" of everyday life. They describe it using several key metaphors, such as transitivity, porosity, rhythm, and footprint.[20] Richard Sennett instead turns porosity into an issue of glamour, an easy topic of discussion in daily newspapers.[21] Wini Mas uses it as a Lego game, a backdrop for workshops and didactic exercises.[22] The latitude and fecundity of the metaphor are also well-illustrated in the book *Porous City*.[23] It is, however, with Secchi and Viganò that porosity becomes a more evident design theme.[24] Not satisfied with Benjamin's interpretation of the Mediterranean city, they investigate the contours of porosity through the physical and mathematical sciences. They use the concept as a descriptor in exploring movements and resistances in nature, the urban environment, and in the social capital anchored to the ground.[25] Compactness and porosity make it possible to elaborate an idea about the future of the contemporary city and a new interpretation of metropolitan territories in which "*le phénomène le plus important devient le mouvement continu des limites de la compacité et de la porosité, la percolation de l'une dans l'autre et la résistance opposée le long d'une série de structures linéaires qui le délimitent*".[26]

The image of the *Ville Poreuse*, developed in studies on Paris, recalls big utopian prefigurations:

"*Une métropole socialement intégrée est une métropole sans barrières physiques, monétaires ou imaginaires qui la compartimentent; une métropole sans enclaves, poreuse, perméable isotrope. L'isotropie, figure par excellence de la démocratie, est la figure qui s'oppose à l'organisation pyramidale et hiérarchisée de la métropole radioconcentrique: localement, elle s'oppose aussi à la métropole multipolaire ou chaque pôle pout générer sa propre périphérie. L'isotropie est évidemment un état idéal au quel on peut tendre; elle n'agit pas de la même manière à toutes les échelles. Nos recherches sur la porosité, la connectivité et la perméabilité montrent que l'obstacle majeur à la représentation d'une métropole isotrope, est la difficulté de sortir d'une imaginaire pour lequel l'ordre, dans tous les domaines, coïncide avec la hiérarchie: hiérarchie dans les espaces verts, dans cours d'eau, dans infrastructures de la mobilité, dans lieux centraux et de la sociabilité, etc. Une idée qui a une origine métaphysique et qui devient opérationnelle à la faveur de la lente construction des États nationaux avec leur centre de pouvoir, leurs bureaucraties et leurs frontiers*".[27]

Urban Interiors cannot ignore the important backdrop created by porosity. But they are not contained within it.[28] They are not part of the grand metaphor. Nor are they a critique of the simplifications with which the season of modernity was re-interpreted, calling on de Certeau and all those we loved for narrating everyday tricks. *Urban Interiors* narrate places of co-belonging of the body and space—with all the relationships of attraction, repulsion, dispossession, exhibition, and conflict they can attribute to themselves. Through these interiors, they reveal a city made up of its exceptions, one in which *intimité* is negotiated with *extimité*. Between voids and solids there are fractured sequences and incomplete, imperfect, and variable states, as when

"*a collapsed void is filled and stretches too quickly due to a sudden input of liquid or air – like a balloon that is suddenly blown up and its parts, which have remained inert for too long and therefore almost glued to one another, do not want to immediately break away ... but are obliged to do so by the force of the air, so they remain here and there, wherever they can, impenetrable ... until the violence of the new pressure stretches them completely".*[29]

I feel the image of the balloon and the irresistible force of the air is appropriate, almost childlike in its simplicity. It is an image by a female writer of visionary verses and prose who always considered the body the core element in her writing.

Holding On to the World

Is the *Wagristoratore*, designed in the late twenties by Piero Portaluppi, an *Urban Interior*?[30] It is undoubtedly not very urban, as it was materialised at 2,300 metres above sea level along the St. James Pass in Val Formazza: two railway carriages, each resting on six pilasters placed symmetrically on either side of a small building. It is a surreal design that is also many different things: an ironic gesture towards Le Corbusier's *machines à habiter*; a cinematographic challenge achieved more by the transportation of the carriages to the pass than their position; an homage to the infrastructural works of the Impresa Girola, who was Portaluppi's partner at the time; a warm, hospitable restaurant for the first tourists to own an automobile, to whom the Milanese architect had already dedicated the modern, extensively equipped hotel over the cascades of the Toce river. Railway carriages condemned to paradoxical immobility, destroyed by Italian partisans escaping towards Switzerland. It is all this rolled into one, plus the cracks that reveal the reality of the new elites, of businesses and technological challenges.

Security Zone is a performance based on trust. It talks, literally, about being held by another. Since the sixties, Vito Acconci has experimented with probable interrelations by observing, stalking, spying on, and bumping into people he meets by chance: at the corner of a street, on a pier, in a museum. Each is an action totally deprived of institutionalised canons, one which involves oblivious passers-by and becomes a way to hold onto the world. He had read the first sociological studies by Erving Goffman, who was almost unknown at the time.[31] *Security Zone* takes place on Pier 18 in New York on 28 February 1971, a wharf lapped by the currents and lashed by icy winds. Acconci is blindfolded, his ears are plugged, and his hands are tied behind his back; he moves in a precarious and dangerous *Urban Interior*, placing his trust in the person guiding him. In Dewey's words, what is visible here is the loyalty in the transactional relationship.[32]

Around the same time, Marco Ferreri was playing with other domains: the surreal western. In *Touche pas à la femme blanche*,[33] an inexhaustible cinematographic and political parody of General Custer's defeat at Little Big Horn, he created an astonishing, dilated *Urban Interior* in the centre of Paris, or rather in the "hole" of Les Halles. The cast is, as we say in these cases, outstanding: Marcello Mastroianni, Catherine Deneuve, Michel Piccoli, Philippe Noiret, Alain Cuny, Serge Reggiani, Ugo Tognazzi, Darry Cowl, and Paolo Villaggio. The film was shot in a huge interior dug out of the city after the demolition of Les Halles, which became part of the story. In this case, the negative of urban space—its reverse—provides a hold on the world. An interior with many stories: the defeat of the Indians during the American epic and the removal of the lower classes from the centre of Paris; actors in period costumes and actors wearing contemporary clothing; the boundaries of the city and the gaping hole in the centre. It is a relentless overflowing of one meaning into another, of one time period into another, in a game of repeated anachronisms. In the first few shots General Terry and American politicians are in a Parisian café discussing the damage wrought by the massive presence of Indians from several tribes; they decide to call General Custer to remedy the situation. In the end the victorious Indians pour in, galloping hell for leather through the contemporary city.

The *Wagristoratore*, *Security Zone,* and *Touche pas à la femme blanche* provide sarcastic, ironic, and paradoxical interpretations of big *Urban Interiors*. They use space and the holds they provide to narrate bodies and their stories. They are exceptions within ordinariness. *Urban Interiors* become special places: the railway carriage and its tracks, repositioned between the gentians of Alpine meadows; the mobile pier, unattached and uncertain under one's feet, where it is possible to experiment with trust while facing a dangerous situation; the gaping hole in the city floor that turns into a contradictory and anachronistic crossroads. However, quite apart from the imaginary space of artistic practices, how useful are *Urban Interiors*?

Let's go back to the city. We are used to all the things that don't work very well in our cities; all the inconveniences and lacking answers. Our everyday life is riddled with minor setbacks. We can all tell personal stories about the problems of public services for which there are far too few resources and ideas and far too little commitment. Our rights to either move or stay are restricted by contingencies that could be removed almost effortlessly. Conflicts, inequalities, and injustice are continuously generated by different forms of coexistence, whether by our own small circle of a few friends or neighbours or by forms that are dramatic, imposed, and overwhelming. Our cities have inured us to crises. Something goes wrong all the time. Inconveniences, hurdles, deadlocks, loss of energies and time. It's always possible to list a city's problems—a list that sometimes becomes a rather trite but successful weapon in political battles. But what if we were to reverse our point of observation and ask different questions of the city? What if we were to pursue what *doesn't* get jammed? What if, in the middle of everything that fuels our indignation and anger towards the city, we pursue what functions regularly rather than what functions once in a blue moon?

63

Urban Interiors are not big public spaces. They are often small, neglected corners. They don't appear to need a lot of attention or resources. But they function: they render the presence of reciprocally intertwined bodies and relationships visible. Every day. Repeatedly. Perhaps not always in the same place. But they compensate for things in the city that function very little, or don't function all. They are places where we can be alone, find ourselves, and reveal ourselves. They provide us with a different idea of the city. A city that functions in normal and anything-but-banal spaces, as I've tried to point out. The normality of urban space is a subject examined at length by Bernardo Secchi.[34] I believe that *Urban Interiors*, sequences of voids and solids in the body of the city, are a good example of normality. Design should know when to stop when faced with these hidden resources. They are resources for the way in which we inhabit the city; for the hidden dynamism which, if truth be told, reveals how the crumbs of rights and democracy can wiggle into spaces, norms, ordinances, and directives. The paradoxical reversal of the luxurious real-estate lobbies studied by Charles Rice.

There's one last point I'd like to emphasise: *Urban Interiors* should be interpreted separately from any notion of plan or order defined, once and for all, by ambiguous spatial figures. And also separately from trust in spontaneity, self-organisation, and that inexhaustible attraction for *mētis*: tricks. They deny the deny both the former and the latter as a backdrop; deny the anonymous and bureaucratic backdrop of norms simply because they often violate them. They deny the messy backdrop of self-organisation that takes itself too seriously, and often provides disappointing results. They are normal spaces because they speak of the order of the body. We feel it is normal for them to be there; they work and we find them. We can discard them easily, without worrying about their demise. There is no algid "public domain" that will shatter, because these places, as I've said repeatedly, have to do with relationships between bodies (alliances, complicity, contrast, and opposition). They enable the communication of an experience, feeling, and meaning; the perception of the city from the viewpoints of *intimité* and *extimité*. They probably facilitate its ordinary confusion. But, perhaps and just as probably, an increase rather than decrease in the confusion of the city may be a positive occurrence.[35]

Notes

1   Jean-Luc Nancy, *Il corpo dell'arte*, Milano: Mimesis, 2014: 12

2   Charles Rice, *Interior Urbanism: Architecture, John Portman and Downtown America*, London: Bloomsbury Academic, 2016; Rice initially started to toy with this idea when studying Benjamin and inhabited space. See *The Emergence of the Interior: Architecture, Modernity, Domesticity*, London and New York: Routledge, 2007. See also: Mark Pimlott, *Without and Within: Essays on Territory and Interior*, Rotterdam: Educational Studies Pr, 2007; Lieven De Cauter, *The Capsular Civilization: on the City in the Age of Fear*, Rotterdam: Nai Publisher, 2004

3   For example: *OASE#101: Microcosm: Searching for the City in Its Interiors* issue edited by Christoph Grafe et al., Rotterdam: NAI 010 Publisher, (2019)

4   Olga Guelf, "The Airconditioned Hanging Garden", editorial in the journal *Interior*, 1965, cited in Rice, *Interior Urbanism*, cit: 69

5   Reference has already been made to Hall's study of anthropology: *The Hidden Dimension*, New York: Anchor Books Editions, 1969. The book has a preface by Umberto Eco; Edward T. Hall, *La dimensione nascosta*, Milano: Bompiani, 1968

6   Gutman's scientific field is that of the relations between public policies, architecture, and social behaviour. With the support of the National Science Foundation, he worked with Robert Geddes and Suzanne Keller in the seventies to create the pioneering study on "The Behavioral Assessment of the Built Environment". The studies performed during that period became well-known: *Neighborhood, City and Metropolis* with David Popenoe, New York: Random House, 1970; *People and Buildings*, New York: Basic Books, 1972 (which quickly became a classic), *The Design of American Housing*, New York: Publishing Centre for Cultural Resources, 1985. Herbert Gans was also one of the most influential sociologists of his generation and President of the American Sociological Association.

7   Jean-Luc. Nancy, *Il corpo dell'arte*, cit: 12. Translated from the Italian.

8   *Urban Interiors. Un'altra forma dello spazio pubblico*, exhibition in Turin, Festival Architettura in Città, 24–27 May 2017, Spazio Q35, via Quittengo 35. See also Cristina Bianchetti, *Spazi che contano*, Roma: Donzelli, 2016: 51 et ff.

9   One of the meanings of the concept of *dispossession* explored by Judith Butler and Athena Athanasiou in *Dispossession: The Performative in the Political*, Malden: Polity Press, 2013. See below in chapter 7. Dispossession does not simply involve more or less authoritarian or paternalistic control-appropriation, but also the delicate and unstable balance between autonomy and subjugation; autonomy that (also) unfolds in this movement from *intimité* to *extimité*. So the *extimité* I talk about later is a form of "dispossession" of intimacy.

10 Alienated (*entfremdet*) is the adjective used by Lacan to discuss the nature of what is foreign at the centre of my being:

Jacques Lacan, *The Seminar, Book VII. The Ethics of Psychoanalysis, 1959–1960*, Jacques-Alain Miller (ed.), New York: Norton & Co., 1992

11 This is the topic of the phenomenology of perception. Maurice Merleau-Ponty, *Phenomenology of Perception*, London: Routledge, 2002 (first ed. 1945)

12 Bianchetti, *Spazi che contano*, cit.

13 Jean-Paul Sartre, *Being and Nothingness: an Essay on Phenomenological Ontology*, New York: Philosophical Library, 1956: 461

14 Jacques Lacan, *The Seminar, Book VII. The Ethics of Psychoanalysis, 1959–1960*, cit.

15 Pier Luigi, "Un pensiero per l'architettura" in *Lotus* no. 151, (2012), 4–5

16 Taking the terms from Gregory Bateson who in the eighties became quite popular within our disciplines (and not only for his aura of anti-psychiatry): *Steps to an Ecology of Mind: Collected Essays in Anthropology, Psychiatry, Evolution, and Epistemology*, Chicago: University of Chicago Press, 1972 and *Mind and Nature: A Necessary Unity (Advances in Systems Theory, Complexity, and the Human Sciences)*, New York: Hampton Press, 1979

17 The topic of borders, boundaries, and separations is one of the topics that, in practice, are never-ending. See one of the last contributions: the monographic issue of *Lotus*, "Borders", no. 168, (April 2019)

18 This is the most frequently cited excerpt of the essay by Benjamin and Lācis: Walter Benjamin and Asja Lācis, "Naples" in *Reflections: Essays, Aphorisms, Autobiographical Writings*, Peter Demez (ed.), New York, 1978: 163–173

19 Martin Mittelmeier, *Adorno a Napoli. Un capitolo sconosciuto della filosofia europea*, Milano: Feltrinelli, 2019

20 Ash Amin and Nigel Thrift, *Cities. Reimagining the Urban*, Cambridge: Polity Press, 2001

21 Richard Sennett, "The World wants more porous cities – so why don't we build them?" In *The Guardian*, (27 November 2015), https://www.theguardian.com/cities/2015/nov/27/

delhi-electronic-market-urbanist-dream

22 *Porous City. How Porous Could the City Become?*, (Fall 2012/2013) @ TU Delft. https://thewhyfactory.com/education/porous-city/ and https://www.mvrdv.nl/projects/179/porous-city-lego-towers

23 Sophie Wolfrum et al (eds.), *Porous City. From Metaphor to the Urban Agenda*, Basel: Birkhäuser, 2018

24 Although there are others, reference is here made only to the main texts that continuously refine their reasoning on this topic: Bernardo Secchi and Paola Viganò. "Opere recenti. Porosità e isotropia", in *Anfione e Zeto*, no. 25, (2014); Ibid., *La ville poreuse*, Genève: Mētis Presses, 2011; Paola Viganò "The Metropolis of the XXIst Century. The Project of a Porous City", OASE 80, (2009), 91–107

25 The following is part of the Territorial Plan of the Salento region, demonstrating latitude in the use of the metaphor: "The porous Salento territory, offering a diffuse spatial capital supporting settlements, multiple ecologies and agricultural productivity, a high quality of landscape and life, through incremental, low, and decentralized investments, seemed to us to project a process of modernization containing an innovative vision for its future." Paola Viganò, *Porosity: Why this Figure is Still Useful*, in *Porous City. From Metaphor to the Urban Agenda*, cit.: 51

26 Ivi: 21

27 Ivi: 22

28 Ernst Bloch probably comes the closest to this concept; he reconnects porosity to interiors and the public dimension, to the relationships between bodies and their friction in space within processes that are often conflictual. Ernst Bloch, "Italien und die Porosität" in *Literarische Aufsätze*, Frankfurt am Main: Suhrkamp Verlag, 1985: 508–515

29 Patrizia Cavalli, *Con passi giapponesi*, Torino: Einaudi, 2018: 133

30 Roberto Dulio, "Società Alberghi della Formazza", in *Piero Portaluppi. Linea errante nell'architettura del Novecento*, Luca Molinari and Fondazione Piero Portaluppi (eds.), Milano: Skira, 2003: 56–59

31 Erving Goffmann, *The presentation of self in everyday life*, Social Science Research Centre: University of Edinburgh, 1956. Research commissioned by the University of Hamburg, still online at https://monoskop.org/images/1/19/Goffman_Erving_The_Presentation_of_Self_in_Everyday_Life.pdf; this precedes *Relations in Public*, New York: Basic Books, 1971.

32 John Dewey and Arthur F. Bentley, *Knowing and the Known*, Boston: Beacon Press, 1949. The transactional relationship is also present in Pier Luigi Crosta's considerations on the forms of relationships in our disciplines.

33 *Touche pas à la femme blanche*, directed by Marco Ferreri, Italo-French production, 1974, 108'

34 Bernardo Secchi, "La città normale" in Dunia Mitter (ed.), *La città reticolare e il progetto moderno*, Novara: CittaStudi, 2008: 47–58

35 Francesco Indovina, *Ordine e disordine nella città contemporanea*, Milano: Franco Angeli, 2017

THE STAMP OF
THE BODY

Structure is harmony,
cohesion: it is how things
work or fit together.
Hertzberger, 2015[1]

Supports and People[2]

Even structuralism ran its course. There was a time when it offered good guarantees. The idea that every element could be conceived of not just for its own sake, but as part of a system based on the relationships between elements, was in itself an expression of value.[3] And since all other ideas were rejected in advance, no work considered structuralist—no architecture, novel, or theory—could be judged to be mediocre, boring, or flawed. It was the age of the autonomy of the signifier and of open work. So open that, Berardinelli ironically wrote, "entering or exiting ... was more or less indifferent".[4] However, structuralism in architecture was much more than this.[5] It was the construction of entire urban areas starting with the modular study of residential plans and connecting spaces. This approach converged with industrialised construction. It asserted the possibility of building an environment suited to mass society.[6]

John N. Habraken is an atypical structuralist.[7] His book, *De Dragers en de mensen: het einde van de massawoningbouw*,[8] is also atypical, and the postscript to the English version contains an interesting story about the book recounted by the author. The first time it was published in the Netherlands in 1961, the book had no illustrations or drawings. However, it soon caught the attention of a group of Dutch architects, who provided Habraken with the resources he needed and encouraged him to start a study to create support structures: the *dragers* in the title. In 1964, the Order of Architects invited ten professional studios to a cycle of conferences to discuss housing problems. It was an opportunity for Habraken to assert his ideas. In 1964 he founded SAR (*Stichting Architecten Research*) which, fifty-four years later, he was to remember as "the first formal architectural research institute".[9] The fact that this may not be true is, all in all, of little importance. The centre studied the residential sector and work focused primarily on what were then considered two key issues: methodology and experimentation. In 1972, Habraken published his book in English with the title *Supports: an Alternative to Mass Housing*. Two years later, in 1974, the book was published in Italian in the Saggiatore series, directed by Giancarlo De Carlo, with the title *Strutture per una residenza alternativa*. The cover no longer contained the words *supports* or *dragers*. The back cover, written by Giancarlo De Carlo (as was the case for all the books in the series) explains the reason for this translation:

"There is an extremely important difference from the concept developed in the twenties and thirties by the architects of Rationalism … It no longer means proposing finite methodologies for uses relating to normalised sets of requirements, but providing frames with the static and engineering features required for the consistency of the housing unit and with a code regulating the insertion of additional elements. It's no longer the plan that commands, but the "support", with the information required to complete it … In terms of production it means replacing the overall construction of already-aggregated systems with a procedure that makes it possible to separate what is permanent from what is variable, maintaining the former at the worksite and delegating the latter to industry. Finally, in terms of use, the prospect of freely varying the inserts enables the possible involvement of users".

Habraken wrote the book not only to promote the design of support structures, but also to find a way for the user, the person who was to live in the house, to play an active role in the building process. This required a complete review of the design process.

The support is a sustaining structure: it facilitates the insertion of housing units that can be placed side by side, modified, and replaced irrespective of one another. Habraken wrote that supports were like bookcases with books we can reposition; they contain housing units which are also, in their own way, mobile and replaceable (although he makes no reference to Le Corbusier's famous bottle holder). Supports are suspended ribbons with the same nature as roads. Like roads, they are fixed and permanent. In essence, they duplicate the ground. The idea is very similar to that of the *Ville Spatiale*, even if nothing suggests the infinite continuity or imaginative force of the latter, against which Habraken sets a convinced principle of realism. He talks about ribbon structures with consistent sections, starting with vertical towers: "support crowns" that create islands removed from heavy traffic and provide a more domestic and comfortable environment. "The support town does not have to be determined in advance: it can be cultivated".[10] These few words reflect the enormous difference with the *Ville Spatiale*.

The supports sustain independent dwellings that can be built, altered, and taken down independently of the others: the end result of catalogue prefabrication (reference is often made to the production of cars). Dwellers can choose their own space, just as consumers can choose what they want to buy. Allowing the dwellers to be involved wasn't initially a big deal: we might say it was a little like choosing a washing machine. Habraken gave an indifferent answer: "a population will get the city it deserves".[11] His vison is poles apart from the modernist furor for a better city, without any veiled or explicit pedagogical goal.

There are no references in the book. Habraken only briefly mentions Eliot Noyes and Buckminster Fuller (but no specific projects) in giving us a glimpse of the direction he is taking. He is not interested in formal results; he seeks other ways of demonstrating the importance of the idea. Francesco Tentori, who wrote the introduction to the Italian version, considered the distinction between the support and the detachable units to express the power of decision and its limitations: "if an individual can make decisions about one element, that is the detachable unit – if not, it is support".[12] The topic of who in the city has the power to decide is present throughout the book.

Habraken returns to his design methodology in several later contributions,[13] defining zones, margins, and rules for creating supports. At this point everything becomes a mathematical game. A strictly deductive game: given certain associations, we can prefigure the result fairly accurately. This is the appeal of firm, clear-cut, transparent, and reassuring rationality. We could say that these were the "other sixties", the ones in which the dreams of cybernetics sank their roots. Every decision had to be argued for or refuted according to how much freedom it eliminated: once a decision was taken, some things were no longer possible. This was the methodology: a system of sequential exclusions.

Mass Housing

Choosing a house is a little like choosing a washing machine: it starts with spatial prefiguration by public authorities and then gives the market—in other words, the producers of "catalogue" houses—free rein. There's nothing very original in that, even if a much more interesting position emerges between the lines of the book: a harsh criticism of the traditional mass housing system and the city it creates. Habraken criticises uniformity as an attack on the occupants' ability to freely express their desires. He writes that uniformity is unacceptable, and even more so if it is imposed by the market or by housing production systems. He touches here on an unsolvable aporia in his own reasoning. It's important to focus on the terms Habraken uses: uniformity is such that, in itself, individual action is manifest as "unnatural", "the disruption of the natural relationship", "the exclusion of the action of individual man".[14] Many years later, in a collected volume on Jaap Bakema's work, he wrote an interview eloquently entitled "The lure of bigness"[15] where he focused extensively on this issue, saying that the (sought-after) prospect of neighbourhoods aging without becoming obsolete depended on solutions that are the opposite of the mass housing system.

Timing is an important issue. Habraken considered mass housing an emergency measure that had continued for far too long and created seriality and determinism. It trapped hundreds of people in a single typological solution—harsh criticism of the glorious aspiration to the *Existenzminimum* and its celebration of productivism. The mass housing system turns housing into a consumer product, establishing in advance what needs it should satisfy and making decisions based on certain economic parameters. It ignores diversified needs, requests that remain unanswered by the products available. Habraken emphasises the antithesis of man and mass residential production; in other words, between the individual and standardised answers to his housing needs. Given the distance between these two aspects of the problem, the solution is the involvement of the dwellers. And not merely their consultation; it is more to do with considering occupants active players in the process. Letting them do something more than just choosing a "catalogue" house. The most interesting aspect of this position, already underscored by De Carlo, is not the process itself (which remains a little vague), but the supporting arguments for it.

Habraken writes about the interdependence between dweller and dwelling. And so, the questions that the mass housing system claimed to have answered once and for all have to be asked again: "What is 'the dwelling'?" "What conditions are to be satisfied by the dwelling we want to make to fulfil its purpose?"[16] The passage is astonishing; it is also an early indication of the best thinking on this issue[17] in that Habraken adds that this question is not the right question. It should be replaced by: "the act of dwelling determines what a dwelling is".[18]

What is "the dwelling"? What can it do? Not *what is it* or *what should it do*, in relation to functional, hygienic, economic, and social parameters, for which the role of the house solves the binomial: to serve; to belong. But rather, *what is it able to do?* There is no bureaucratic, regulatory, or functional dimension. Nor are there any models for this. What a house can do depends on how the occupant relates to it, through considerations, decisions, and actions that are his alone and cannot be generalised.[19] They involve his ability to satisfy his own needs by acting and inhabiting. In other words, they involve assessing and choosing countless little details; expressing preferences regarding his desires, expectations, personal convictions, tastes, and imagination. They express the resolve and freedom to either emulate others or to do better. To act only temporarily or to imagine oneself in the story of one's own individual or shared experience of dwelling over a much longer period. Following a trend or, on the contrary, moving away from it. Looking for a suitable environment where one can do what one wants: an inviolable environment. A person's housing choice (Habraken's words) reflect "[one's] position in life". An anti-functionalist approach *par excellence* that once again echoes the statement at the root of the matter: "a population will get the city it deserves". Without being excessively worried about ephemeral, ordinary, and banal gestures; with ludic consumption and fragile performances. Without the modernist conscience that pursues the best form: "a population will get the city it deserves".

The answer to the question—*what can the dwelling do?*—led Habraken to express considerations surprisingly similar to the ones formulated roughly thirty years later regarding the landscape of dispersion and its innovatory settlement configuration in Europe. Here too it involved "doing one's thing", either to emulate or do better than others, to reflect oneself in one's dwelling, or to display "a real passion for diversity".[20] It's important to stress that Habraken was referring to high-density urban territories with numerous infrastructures—the exact opposite of the frayed edges of dispersed European cities. And remember, he was writing at least twenty years before postmodernism and its impetuous return to the individual, sense of place, and history.

The Stamp—Familiar and Unfamiliar

So, what can a house do? Owning a house is closely linked to action. Inhabiting means acting to attain, but it doesn't end in the right to property—the real pulsating core regulating the relationship between man and objects. An almost-pragmatic Habraken adds that one of the positive characteristics of our existence is the fact that satisfying certain needs requires a commitment on our part; a personal, creative action. It's not the finished product or its quality that is interesting, but the possibility to act, to do it our way, a way we consider useful, beautiful, and convenient; to do so either by following other people or by setting ourselves apart from them.

When there is a dramatic lack of resources, involving occupants is part of the act of inhabiting rather than a necessary remedy to that lack. It has a nuance that Habraken doesn't hesitate to define as civil: building houses is a civil action *par excellence*. In other words, it is emancipation through housing. Not through property, as mentioned earlier, but through an action performed by the occupant. Habraken goes on to write that it is a simple position which nevertheless sparked a strong reaction from architects convinced they had the right and moral obligation to control all aspects of a project in order to achieve the best results. Or who, more simply, were unable to imagine any other way.

In the eyes of these architects, the moral dimension involves duty; chiefly public and professional duty. Habraken reverses the perspective: he considers the house from the viewpoint of an active individual who can solve his problems through interaction and has to put himself out there in the world: "To possess something we have *to take it* in our hand, touch it, test it, put our stamp on it".[21] Here he introduces the corporeal, tacit, affective, qualitative dimension of action. Stamps are one of the central images in his thoughts about the body. A body that touches and is touched; one that finds itself by experiencing the hardness or ductility of what it presses against. A body that acquires knowledge through the hand with which it touches, revealing the resistance of objects and leaving an impression on them.

"Objects bear the impressions of our hands, the marks of our eyes, and the outline of our experiences".[22] It is the body that breathes life into objects. We affect objects as much as they affect us. Roberto Esposito makes this the core issue in his book and recalls the relevant philosophical traditions. Habraken said that "something becomes our possession because we make a sign on it, because we give it our name, or defile it, because it shows traces of our existences".[23] Stamps are the crossroads at which the lives of objects (and houses) are interwoven with our body. And this is why individuals create and introduce chaos in the mass housing system—or, annihilated, exit the system overwhelmed. Because it is a body. It acts and is acted upon. It is able to leave impressions. It cannot be "reduced in essence, to a statistic".[24]

Habraken is crystal-clear about this. And it is here, rather than in his ribbon-shaped bottle holder, that, in my opinion, he takes a giant leap forward in his reasoning. A leap that leads to another issue (although without developing it): familiarity is recalled by leaving a stamp, by acting, by putting oneself out there in the world, and by acquiring knowledge. Our familiarity with objects and spaces is a practical attitude: we know how to act with them. Not with objects in general, but with these specific objects.[25] We could review the entire design culture from this angle: from the de-familiarisation of modern design, which separates subject and space through its algid approach, to the reappropriation of the familiar in the sixties and seventies, the years of the famous *as found*,[26] and to daily life in inhabitable spaces pursued by so many studies in the ensuing twenty years.

Habraken provides a specific overture to this story, more through his emphasis on the notion of impression than for his excellent later work on the "structure of the ordinary": his was one of the most meticulous studies on the built environment and its individual organisation published in the late nineties.[27] However, it was in his reflections thirty years earlier that the Dutch architect introduced the issue of familiarisation as the transformation of space vis-à-vis the body.

Habraken is an unusual structuralist, because if it is true that "structuralism does have something to do with structure, but just as much with freedom",[28] it is also true that this freedom is understood similarly to Chomsky's language game or generative grammar. Instead, however, Habraken focuses on the freedom of the living body dreaming about objects and space, on impressions, and on familiarisation with the world of objects. He highlights the affective and corporeal spaces involved in the social construction of inhabiting. He does it discreetly, almost as if talking about something else, without searching for radical implications. His concern is to distance himself from the mass production that generates suffering and alienation. His is also an unusual structuralism from another perspective, as the body in the structuralist experience is usually a removed body.

Nevertheless, the wind changed direction in the mid-eighties. And not just for architecture and urbanism. Semiology and theory of structure became first imperceptibly and then visibly weakened, even in the fields in which they had been strongest. Their greatest supporters withdrew to more circumscribed fields, leaving behind all the fanfare that, for a few decades, had led to widespread infatuation.

"We thought we were part of a revolution, but instead we were already shifting to a new regime of modernity guaranteed by university and cultural institutions. By the aesthetic theories of the modern, now consolidated and protectively dedicated to supporting the dissemination of what appeared to be outrageous only a few decades earlier. We thought we were still in an extremist situation, but instead we had shifted to one of neo-classicism".[29]

Notes

1 Herman Hertzberger, *Architecture and Structuralism. The Ordering of Space*, Rotterdam: Nai010, 2015: 32

2 John Habraken, "The lure of bigness", in Dirk van den Heuvel (ed.), *Jaap Bakema and the Open Society*, Amsterdam: Archis Publishers, 2018, 298–300, cit.: 298

3 "There are moments in our life in which the isolation of man from things becomes destroyed: in that moment we discover the wonder of relationship between man and things …. For us in CIAM the relations between things and within things are of greater importance than the things themselves." This citation from Jaap Bakema at the VIII CIAM 1951 in Hoddesdon, "The heart of the city", can be found in Tomas Valena, "From Deep Structure to Spatial Practice", in Tomas Valena, Tom Avermaete and Georg Vrachliotis, *Structuralism Reloaded. Rule-Based Design in Architecture and Urbanism*, London: Axel Menges, 2011, 124–133, cit.: 124

4 Alfonso Berardinelli, *Casi critici*, Macerata: Quodlibet, 2007: 133

5 Robert Banham, *Megastructure – Urban Futures of the Recent Past*, London: Thames and Hudson, 1976; *Structuralism Reloaded. Rule-Based Design in Architecture and Urbanism*, cit. Hertzberger, *Architecture and Structuralism. The Ordering of Space*, cit.

6 Monique Eleb, "Reinventer l'habiter du 'plus grand nombre'", in Jean-Louis Cohen and Vanessa Grossman (eds.), *Une architecture de l'engagement 1960–1985*; in AUA, Paris: La Découvert, 2015: 52–62; Thomas Köhler and Ursula Müller (eds.), *Radically Modern. Urban Planning and Architecture in 1960s*, Berlin: Wasmuth & Zohlen, 2015

7 Tomas Valena, "Structural Approaches and Rule-Based Design in Architecture and Urban Planning", in Valena, Avermaete and Vrachliotis, *Structuralism Reloaded. Rule-Based Design in Architecture and Urbanism*, cit.: 6–19; Koos Bosma, Dorin van Hoogstraten and Martijn Vos, *Housing for the Millions: John Abraken and the SAR (1960–2000)*, Rotterdam: NAI, 2000; John N. Habraken et al. (eds.), *Variations*, Cambridge: MIT Press, 1976; John N. Habraken, Andrés Mignucci and Jonathan Teicher, *Conversation*

with Form: a Workbook for Students of Architecture, London: Routledge, 2014

8   John N. Habraken De Dragers en de mensen: het einde van de massawoningbouw, Rotterdam: NAI, 1961; English trans.: Supports: an alternative to mass housing, London: The Architectural Press, 1972; Italian trans.: Strutture per una residenza alternativa, Milano: Il Saggiatore, 1974

9   Habraken, "The lure of bigness", cit.: 298

10 Habraken, Supports: an alternative to mass housing, cit.: 73

11 Ivi: 81–82

12 Ivi: 26

13 John N. Habraken, Three R's for Housing, Amsterdam: Scheltema-Holkema, 1970, in Forum, vol. XX, no 1, (1966). The most important books by Habraken can be found at https://www.habraken.com/html/on_housing.htm

14 Habraken, Supports: an alternative to mass housing, cit.: 21

15 Habraken, "The lure of bigness", cit.

16 Habraken, Supports: an alternative to mass housing, cit.: 16–17

17 I am thinking here of the works by Antonio Tosi on housing and its policies that have become classics: Ideologie della casa, Milano: Franco Angeli, 1984; Abitanti, Bologna: Il Mulino, 1994; and those that are more recent: Case, quartieri, abitanti, politiche, Milano: Clup, 2004; Le case dei poveri, Milano: Mimesis, 2016

18 Habraken, Supports: an alternative to mass housing, cit.: 16

19 These excerpts and those that follow are in Habraken's book on p. 14

20 Cristina Bianchetti, "Abitare l'Adriatico: nuove linee di ricerca", in Pepe Barbieri, Alberto Clementi (eds.), Territori Flusso. SS16 e Ipercittà adriatica, Trento: List Lab, 2014, 34–36, cit.: 35. The book revisits, after ten years, the considerations in Cristina Bianchetti, Abitare la città contemporanea, Milano: Skira, 2003

21 Habraken, Supports: an alternative to mass housing, cit.: 12

22 Roberto Esposito, Le persone e le cose, Torino: Einaudi, 2014: 93

23 Habraken, Strutture per una residenza alternativa, cit.: 12

24 Ivi: 8

25 Issue often referred to by Pier Luigi Crosta, starting with his studies on Laurent Thévenot.

26 Claude Lichtenstein and Thomas Schregenberger (eds.), As found. The Discovery of the Ordinary: British Architecture and Art of the 1950s, Zürich: Lars Müller Publishers, 2001

27 John N. Habraken, The Structure of the Ordinary. Form and Control in the Built Environment, Cambridge London: MIT Press, 1998

28 Hertzberger, Architecture and Structuralism. The Ordering of Space, cit.: 36

29 Berardinelli, Casi critici, cit.: 99

THE LIBERATED BODY

*Les rapports de pouvoir passent
à l'intérieur des corps.*
Foucault, 1977[1]

Irony That Isn't Funny

Manfredo Tafuri's opinion on "radical architecture" is notorious and *tranchant*: that it is irony that isn't funny. As in previous chapters, I will focus on well-studied issues and assess them from my own point of view. I will also avoid alluding to the problem of the roots of Florentine experimentalism in the sixties, an ostensibly never-ending topic about which everyone wishes to have their say (facilitated by the numerous discordant self-presentation strategies implemented by Archizoom and Superstudio[2]). All I need to do is follow the impressions left behind by bodies that live in the continuous, homogeneous, palaeo-technical space of their visionary urban prefigurations—entrusted to montages, studio drawings, and, more generally, to a language borrowed from cartoons and consisting of "vignettes inhabited by neo-primitive bodies"; free bodies in the nakedness that belonged to the environment before it was ever theirs. A mix of populist anarchism and the liberatory instances of May 1968 in France[3]—or, if you prefer, one of the many examples of syncretism that combines everything and is behind the myth of radical architecture: Panzieri and Benevolo; La Pira and Tronti; critiques of capitalistic exploitation and fashionable meeting places; the "wild reality of the working class"; and the little villas built in the countryside around Florence.

Let's go back to bodies. The five videos developed by Superstudio in 1972, *Five Fundamental Acts*, focus on the relationship between architecture and life actions. Parts of the storyboard were published in *Casabella* (1972–73), while the first video, *Life Supersurface*, was shown at the exhibition entitled "The New Domestic landscape: Achievements and Problems of Italian Design" held at the MoMA in 1972.[4] *Supersurface* is "the 'total city' as an energy and communications network".[5] In the photomontage by Superstudio, the bodies of children playing, animals grazing, and adults walking or holding hands with their backs to the spectator are placed on an anonymous, smooth, chequered floor reflecting the sky of the *Supersurface*. It would be ungenerous to point out that they all have young, beautiful, white bodies. It is more relevant to say they are bodies free to move within an invisible energy information network. The image I consider emblematic of this discussion is in this first video; it shows a young man and woman with their backs towards an adolescent cradling a small child, and another three children, a little older, crouched in front, mimicking the primary group and its reproductive requirements rather than any kind of family.[6] The landscape is a nondescript flat surface stretching to the hills in the distance. Behind the group there is a tent: a shelter or dome, indicating an attempt or the desire to control the environment with very few means.[7] Half-naked, happy, smiling bodies. A group photo. The postures and gazes have something in common with those in Cartier Bresson's very beautiful photographs of communities in New Mexico taken in the early seventies.[8] The same young people, the same children, the small, dilated, empowered bodies free from chemical substances, spiritualisms, and with faith in the community and in their own rebellion. Will the limitless, nondescript, and indifferent city typical of "radical architecture" settle in the small communities of Drop City or Arcosanti? In the background are reflections of the vernacular American landscape prepared in the fifties by the extraordinary John Brinkerhoff Jackson.[9]

Cartier Bresson's photographs raise the question of the relationships between radical architecture in the early seventies and American counterculture. It's true that the Italian radicals distanced themselves from American youth culture as much as they did from the European Frankfurt-style models of the late sixties ("better Mohammedanism preaching holy war, than pacifist Buddhism"[10]). But it is just as true that their photomontages also contain groups of young hippies. It's not a question of sources or citations, which are indeed present (Superstudio used references to young hippies at the concerts in Woodstock or the Isle of Wight to affirm that the densification or dispersion of urban life was not linked to three-dimensional structures, i.e., to architecture).[11] Neither is it a question of sources or citations, nor a question of genealogies, traditions, or influences, but rather one of differences between symbolic structures and imaginative backgrounds.

Drugs, Zen, spiritualisms, and liberated bodies de-dramatised the modern with new ways of being in small groups. When did all this end? In Italy, the peak of the presence of the happy and slightly bewildered bodies of counter-culture was the exact moment it began to decline. It felt as if counterculture had been revived, but also died: the festivals organised by the magazine *Re Nudo* in Milan in 1974, 1975, and 1976 were the final reruns. Hundreds of young people gathered in Parco Lambro for the most important musical event of that period, which was preceded by the great music festivals of the sixties in England and America. Here too, the body was a forceful key player. *Nudi verso la follia* ("Naked towards madness") was the title of the documentary by Angelo Rastelli about the last edition of the event (1976). *"When referring to that period, it's easy to treat it all as a delirium … if you don't consider the strength of their feeling of being masters of their fate. Active, not passive. Part of a real movement".*[12]

Liberated bodies participating in their consecration by tackling all sorts of conflicts: the festival was not just about music, harmony, evasion, and conciliation, it was also an ensemble of big and small controversies over food, the way the festival was organised, and the need to limit the use of drugs, as well as of conflicts between men and women, between heterosexuals and homosexuals. Forty years later, in 2016, Michele Serra wrote an article in the magazine *L'Espresso* entitled "Quando al Parco Lambro finì il futuro" ("When the future ended in Parco Lambro").[13] The subtitle read: "In June 1976 Milan was shocked by the young proletariat's festival organised by the magazine *Re Nudo*. A glorification of absolute freedom that was to mark the end of hope". Serra spoke about bodies incarnating the dwindling hippy soul of the youth movement of the sixties and seventies (which in the USA had already been on its way out for some time): "Forty years ago, the cover of the *L'Espresso* with the photograph of a girl with naked breasts and a boy wearing orange clothes, both with their eyes half closed, in meditation or simply 'stoned': that cover was in honour of the defeated. Because the third festival of the young proletariat in Milan, in June 1976, was the great rite of passage from the years of dreams to the years of lead". Dancing, nudism, music, "peace and love"—a motto that today sounds slightly ridiculous—left the stage to the *bande autonome*.

"Combining the proletarian revolution, journeys to India, the 'barrel' of the shotgun and the 'barrel' of the joint, Mao, and Jerry Rubin was a colossal mistake revealing its fragility and empty chatter. One by one the reference points of

the extremely lively youth counterculture began to falter, a counterculture that emerged in the sixties and exploded in the worldwide turmoil of 1968. One of the first to go was Jerry Rubin, the historic leader of the American movement against the Vietnam war, pacifist, Castroite, alter ego (and predecessor) of Cohn-Bendit and Rudi Dutschke. Rubin was present at Parco Lambro, held conferences, took part in debates, but was almost completely ignored by both the media and participants. Charismatic political leaders were no longer stars; the self-proclaimed and self-invited star in June 1976 was the uncontrollable mass of the participants, a boiling magma, unyielding towards classical politics, and thus to the concept of 'class', and even to the new policy of Marxist groups like Avanguardia Operaia and Lotta Continua, also present at the Festival and immediately blown away by the frenzied masses. It is as if the object of an experiment was slipping through the fingers of its initiators: 'youth proletariat' was like Frankenstein, the creator succumbing to its creature".

How did the brief parabola of American counterculture, with its dilated bodies, enter and modify architectural research, notwithstanding its short and controversial encounter with radical architecture? Historiography focusing on the connection between design culture and the counterculture of the sixties and seventies is fragmented but quite extensive. One of the most recent examples was the exhibition "Hippie Modernism. The Struggle for Utopia" organised by the Walker Art Center, the University of California, and the Berkeley Art Museum in 2016;[14] it proposed a review of the multiple intersections between these two symbolic areas by investigating the traces of another utopia—one other than that of a mass society built on fascination with technologies and the new imperatives of ecology and community. A few years earlier, Caroline Maniaque had based her study on Bernard Huet's concept of *architecture douce*.[15] *Douce* compared to the *rigidité* and *résistance* of the modern, obviously; a vague category that included houses made of recycled materials, huts, shelters, capsules, and ecological sensitivities.[16] Caroline Maniaque studied the way *architecture douce* was disseminated in magazines, studies and didactics. She studied a process that historians call the construction of fame. Attention almost always focuses on the community (small, primitive, self-centred) as well as on the bodies it attracts. All attempts to revive inflatable, organic, flexible, expandable, suspended, and itinerant architectures were ascribed to the influence—if not direct, at least allusive—of counterculture. Prototypes people continued to imagine, before and after the sixties and seventies, as having symbolic and visionary features encroaching on art.[17] Episodes that shared the concept of free housing, deaf to calls for minimalism, neutrality, and purity; housing centred on the body, its habits, desires, and abilities. Colin Ward acknowledged the fact that it lasted for a longer period: Arcadia on the shores of the Thames in the period between the two world wars.[18] The same was acknowledged by Alain Touraine in his essay "Contre-Culture", written for the *Encyclopedia Universalis* in the early seventies and considered, even then, the demarcation line between cultural change and conflict.[19]

Whatever happened to the demand for autonomy, the search for authenticity, freedom, and self-organisation, and the refusal of every hierarchy of counterculture? It was reabsorbed and neutralised within the neoliberal order that was established in the last two decades of the twentieth century. The political dimension of the aesthetic strategies of the sixties goes far beyond irony that isn't funny. If this is the parabola of the values of counterculture, finally absorbed by the same project it wanted to oppose, where is the critique of architecture after that turning-point—which was, in its own way, tragic? At the end of the twentieth century, what remains of those half-naked happy bodies that wanted to de-dramatise the modern? How did architectural and urban planning design culture deal with a disaggregating world and its ensuing effects? The passion for critique in the sixties and seventies was a very intense moment that many still highlight today. It was the phase of "extremism". And then everything started to weaken.

Genealogies: In Search of One's Own History

In the words of Carlo Olmo, one of the strings in that entangled skein was later called *operaismo*,[20] the most blatant and brash trend in Italy that broke with the cultural politics of the Communist Party: Marxist and workers' issues juxtaposed against antifascism and democracy. I'm not interested in the relationship between *operaismo* and radical architecture, which, in my opinion, is superficial and instrumental. I'm more interested in understanding how, at a time when bodies were the cornerstone of the relationship between architectural culture and politics, they disappeared and then re-emerged in the idea of *Multitude*, i.e., of what is acknowledged as contemporary *post-operaismo*.

We could oversimplify and concisely say that, in the sixties and seventies, the search for a direct relationship between intellectuals and the working class was created to contrast with "corporate and productive totality" during the decades of the Golden Age; a contrast also utilised in urban theory.[21] In other words, it was an approach that invested directly in architects, writers, and intellectuals, and turned the city into a battleground for critics. The clash took place primarily in two magazines: *Quaderni Piacentini* and *Quaderni Rossi*, the former more cultural, the latter more political (if this distinction is at all meaningful). Others included *Classe Operaia* and *Contropiano*, but also *Quaderni del territorio* and *Città Classe*. Although these publications were short-lived, they played a significant role in the architectural debate.[22] They were used to launch impassioned appeals as well as "disconsolate, angry" complaints and allegations. Adriano Olivetti was perhaps their most important, and therefore most successful, target. Panzieri, Bellocchio, Fortini, and Tronti. This is the history of Italian culture, which during that period juxtaposed the pride and demands of workers in big factories with the refusal to work, the sabotage of production, and salaries as an independent variable; the goal was to create a convergence between the mass worker and a precarious, unemployed intellectual workforce.

An insurmountable distance existed between the *operaisti* (and their positions) and the traditional left and its organic intellectuals, including quite a few architects. "Organic" as in the view proposed by Antonio Gramsci, who interpreted the intellectual political dimension as the construction of a project for the future; as an assumption of responsibility. That world disintegrated under the impact of impetuous forces during the season of extremisms, of the hard, violent juxtaposition of autonomy and hegemony, of the imperious urgency of a position that developed as a struggle:[23] "Let the intellectuals learn from workers!"[24] Today, many scholars have reviewed the ideas that generated this impact and have reinterpreted Tronti's "workers' science" as hard, elementary, and sharp; the equivalent of the pure working class that was emerging in Turin, the heart and soul of the most important company town in Italy.[25]

A warrior race that had arrived at its appointment with history: the mass worker, unskilled and undisciplined, was the perfect example of the concept of abstract work, of pure expenditure of working energy—and, therefore, had high fighting potential. All this (the distance from Gramsci and Weber, the creation of a new worker-science) was considered a return to authentic Marxist doctrine: to the *true Marx*. It was a thread of the skein that retained its appeal: because its four heroes (Panzieri, Bellocchio, Fortini, and Tronti) were so different, it was possible to foray into unlimited territories in which to lose oneself—from Tronti's *Operai e capitale*, the hub of science-class-fight, to Fortini's *La verifica dei poteri*. There is very little in all that worker furore that is relevant to our perspective. There are the unskilled workers rebelling against capital. There is the "pagan warrior race". There are no bodies, only political categories. This is why the genealogy of the critical philosophy of architecture, which developed along this train of thought, is inapplicable to a discussion on bodies, spaces, and struggles.

The revival of *operaismo* by Antonio Negri and Michael Hardt, using the concept of *Multitude*,[26] is different and yet closely interlinked[27]—even after the dissolution of *operaismo* in the great rift of the eighties that divided everything, weakened everything, and disaggregated everything through what Boltanski and Esquerre called "new economic devices", which at the end of the century were linked to the diversification of goods and values.[28] That's when the critique of Negri's theory became increasingly visionary and gradually brought new concepts into play.[29] *Multitude* is one of these; perhaps the most important. It is the opposite of the mass in the horizon of *One*.[30]

It is the *Multitude* of bodies that live in the global market, suffer its inequalities, and are expropriated from their jobs and even their lives—without an "I" to acquire a dominant position, or to decide to continue the performance. *Multitude* is body in the sense of Spinoza's concept of permanence through change.[31] It is plural. It narrates subversion. Negri writes of the bodies that make up the *Multitude:*[32]

"If I look back on my life, on the life of my generation and that of the generations that lived around the year 1968 and also afterwards, I realise that our experience, for better or for worse, can be summarised as follows: the extreme, non-stop attempt to instil in experience the tradition of singularity against the universal and to stake our bodies against the miserable and now empty statements of all universal essences that are invariably behind all wars and all kinds of destructions".[33]

Multitude "is a demon" to be exorcised precisely because it is "much more powerful than any Universal: humanity, rights, law ...".[34] The political ontology of the West is built around the obsession with *One*. It is within this obsession that modernity creates the Public, the Private, the People, the Individual, and the State. Division, conflict, and struggle are what make up the patterns of being in the world, but the West is permeated by the obsession of reducing it to *One*. It is political ontology. It is Thomas Hobbes' *Leviathan*, where the body of the Sovereign contains all the citizens and reduces them to the People. The position assumed by Negri and Hardt overturns this position. In their considerations, democracy is inscribed in antagonisms even more than it was in the past: the organisational forms of current capitalism (decentralisation of decision-making, flexibility and radical mobility, the interaction of everything with everything) are perceived as the required conditions for democracy, no longer limited to the form of *One*, to that of the power of the sovereign state. Still inscribed in antagonisms like an immanent *telos* of their resolution; made possible by the liberation of a *Multitude* finally able to govern itself.

Negri and Hardt shared Marx's faith that history was on their side with a large group of *post-operaisti* scholars.[35] While Marx's theory was historically associated with the centralised and hierarchically organised automated industrial work of machines, the authors considered that the new hegemony of immaterial labour renewed the credibility of the revolutionary turning point—the potential for which, as in Marx, is inherent in capitalism, in the new gaps between productive forces and relations of production. This is the humus where the seeds of the future create new forms of life; the new *common* that will free people from the old social form.

Hardt and Negri have in mind the protests of the early twenty-first century. In these bodies in revolt they celebrate the rise of a new revolutionary subject. Integrating Deleuze and Foucault, they prefigure a crack in the disciplinary regime governing bodies and a repositioning of the control procedures in a different kind of politics, one which allows more autonomous and independent forms of subjectivity: the invention of new life forms in which subjectivity can freely express and contribute to the formation of new social relations in order to contrast with capital. A position that is still strictly finalist.

Being Visible in Space, Standing Up, Breathing, Moving, Staying Still, Talking, Being Silent...

Yet another thread (although there are many more)[36] twists around collective and transitory forms of protest. The early-twenty-first-century protests studied by feminist literature, referring more specifically to the presence of bodies in defining political action and the public nature of space. Being visible, standing up, breathing, moving, staying still, talking, being silent. Placing one's body in front of another's actions. Refusal to move, refusal to give up one's seat. They are all features of a dual resistance: spatial and corporeal.[37] It's impossible to talk of the body without space, and vice versa.

In other words, it is the staging of bodies-in-place or bodies-out-of-place in space, a characteristic of spontaneous aggregations, public assemblies, crowds, and transitory gatherings as well as of individual action, that acts as a spark for collective movements (Rosa Parks, the African-American civil rights activist who in 1955 refused to give up her seat on the bus to a white man, is perhaps the most well-known example).[38] In these collective actions the body tackles (and draws attention to) several problems: precarity, vulnerability, dispossession, demand for a liveable life, and exclusion from the public sphere of appearance.

"When political struggles emerge … they are mobilising precarity and even sometimes quite deliberately mobilising the public exposure of the body, even when it means being exposed to force, or detention or possibly death. It is not that vulnerability is converted into resistance, at which point strength can triumph over vulnerability. Strength is not exactly the opposite of vulnerability and this becomes clear, I would suggest, when vulnerability is itself mobilised, not as an individual strategy, but in concert. This is probably not what Hannah Arendt had in mind when she said that politics depends on acting in concert – I can't imagine she would have much liked the Slut Walks. But perhaps, if we rethink her view so that the body, and its requirements, becomes part of the action and aim of the political, we can start to approach a notion of "plurality" that is thought combined with both performativity and interdependency".[39]

The spatial aspect is fundamental to this concept of plurality. Bodies come together, move and talk together, demand a certain space insofar as it is public. Space is not already public and acknowledged as such: the very public character of the space is being disputed and fought over. This is what Butler writes, but also what a part of urban theory converges on and anticipates.[40] The plurality of bodies finds and produces the public through occupation and reconfiguration of the material environment—which is also part of action and is re-functionalised in relation to it.

Visibility is crucial. Making oneself visible in space was already a core concept in Arendt's thinking; she wrote of the "space of appearance" generated though political action.[41] Which places the concept outside the realm of an idea that cannot be defined once and for all. Appearance is linked to exposure, to the performative act, and to occupation. In the relationship of critical genealogy that Butler maintains with German philosophy, it seems to me there is another passage: it is visibility that frees us from the omnipotence and fear of power. When, together with Dewey, Habermas, Hirschman,

Sennett, and Mouffe,[42] we lament the poverty of political imagination, the weakening of the public sphere, the shattering of the public, this is what we are talking about: the need to rebuild the collective and political capacity to make power visible. I think that feminist literature adds that all this passes primarily through bodies, conjuring up a dimension that is both individual and collective.[43] We certainly cannot free ourselves from power. But we can ally ourselves in different forms of authority.

Alliances between bodies, the dislocation of bodies, multitudes as forms of permanence in changes: even the "dispossessed" can have a form of agency. They can enter the field of politics. Even life stripped of rights (Arendt and Agamben's *naked life*) is nonetheless likely to get angry and be indignant: it is part of the political domain. Feminist literature considers not only the enhancement of needs, rights, and desires, through the medium of the body, as priorities, but also dispossession, being exposed, affection, expropriation of things, concepts, and ideologies implemented by social norms.[44] A dislocation of political action that finds its material and symbolic centre in the body.

Contrasting with the prophecy of the disappearance of bodies is the sensational entry of the biological horizon into the political horizon, as previously prophesied by Foucault. Politics has a direct relationship with biological life, and this has been a specific consideration even in urban theory.[45] It continues to be a key topic in meetings, books, and discussions that endlessly reformulate Foucault's paradigm vis-à-vis the power exercised on bodies and on the life of the mind, including perception, attention, and memory.[46]

But there is an anything-but-negligible implication: in a bitter note to Butler's book, Roberto Esposito acknowledges that when biological life enters the fray as the object and subject of power, death also enters into the action. He refers to what Butler, in her urgency to testify to this new alliance between bodies, never took into account: the simultaneous unleashing of Jihadist terrorism illuminating the obscure background of that historical period. A dramatic confirmation of the fact that "by always investing more directly in life ... one eventually involves death".[47] An inextricable knot woven in bodies.

"The same dynamics which, for at least a century, have placed the body at the centre of politics have also made it vulnerable ... only a politics of life can fight the politics of death. Spinoza said we do not even know what a body can do. Living bodies need to be mobilised against dead bodies".[48]

Notes

1   Michel Foucault, *Les rapports de pouvoir passent à l'intérieur des corps*, interview with Lucette Finas, in *La Quinzaine Litteraire*, no. 247, 1–15, (January 1977), 4–6

2   Dominique Rouillard, *Superarchitectures. Le future de l'architecture 1950–1970*, Paris: Editions de la Villette, 2004; Roberto Gargiani. *Archizoom Associati, 1966–1973: dall'onda pop alla superficien neutra*, Milano: Electa, 2007; Ibid., *Inside No-Stop City Parking Residientels & Système Climatique Universel*, Paris: B2, 2018

3   Manfredo Tafuri, *History of Italian Architecture. 1945–1985*, Cambridge: MIT Press, 1989. Tafuri writes about an unfamiliarity with the experimentalism of Gruppo 63 that paves the way for "theatres for psychedelic actions in which to drag a mythical proletariat". The image inserted in Tafuri's critique is taken from "No-Stop City. Residential Park. Climatic. Universal System", published in *Design Quarterly*, 78–79, undated (January 1971) and extensively reproduced. For example, on page 205 of the book by Gargiani, Archizoom *Associati, 1966–1973: dall'onda pop alla superficie neutra*, cit. Regarding Archizoom's "political" opinions, see also Pier Vittorio Aureli, *The Project of Autonomy: Politics and Architecture Within and Against Capitalism*, New York: Princeton Architectural Press, 2012

4   Peter Lang and William Menking, *Superstudio. Life Without Objects*, Milano: Skira, 2003: 175

5   Adolfo Natalini, cited in Roberto Gargiani and Beatrice Lampariello, Superstudio, Bari-Roma: Laterza, 2010: 73

6   Ivi: 174. See also: https://www.cristianotoraldodifrancia.it/fundamental-acts-1971-1973/

7   Gargiani and Lampariello, *Superstudio*, cit.: 76

8   Henri Cartier-Bresson, USA. "New Mexico. Near Taos. The Lama Foundation community", 1971, https://pro.magnumphotos.com/C.aspx?VP3=SearchResult&STID=2S5RYDZKI9KP (accessed 4 April 2020)

9   Attilio Petruccioli, *John Brinckerhoff Jackson*, Bari: Icar, 2006

10 The citation is in Gargiani, *Archizoom Associati, 1966–1973: dall'onda pop alla superficie neutra*, cit.: 161

11 Gargiani and Lampariello, *Superstudio*, cit.: 73

12 Angelo Rastelli, *Nudi Verso La Follia - Festival di Parco Lambro 1976* (film/documentary) https://www.youtube.com/watch?v=J-PvmFtHkFk&t=1223s (accessed 4 April 2020)

13 Michele Serra, "Quando al Parco Lambro finì il futuro", *L'Espresso*, (21 June 2016), http://espresso.repubblica.it/visioni/2016/06/20/news/quando-a-parco-lambro-fini-il-futuro-1.273580 The quotes in the text that follow are taken from this article.

14 Andrew Blauvelt (ed.), *Hippie Modernism. The Struggle for Utopia*, Minneapolis: Walker Art Center with the Berkeley Art Museum/Pacific Film Archive, 2016.

15 Caroline Maniaque, *Go West! Des architectes au pays de la contre-culture*, Marseille: Parenthèse, 2014

16 *Architecture douce*, monographic issue of *Architecture d'aujourd'hui*, (June 1975)—a position abandoned the following year when, in the editorial entitled *La nuit américaine* by Bernard Huet in the same magazine, the focus shifted to the influence exerted on big buildings by economic and financial capital. Jean-Louis Cohen, *Scènes de la vie future. L'architecture europénne et la tentation de l'Amérique 1893–1960*, USA: Flammarion, 1994

17 Larry Busbea, *Topologies. The Urban Utopia in France. 1960–1970*, Cambridge: MIT Press, 2007; Gabi Scardi (eds.), *Less. Strategie alternative dell'abitare*, 5 Continents, Milano: PAC, 2006

18 Dennis Hardy and Colin Ward, *Arcadia for All. The Legacy of a Makeshift Landscape*, Nottingham: Five Lives Publications, 2004

19 Cited in Maniaque, *Go West! Des architectes au pays de la contre-culture*, cit.: 18

20 Aureli, *The Project of Autonomy: Politics and Architecture Within and Against Capitalism*, cit. The book Panzieri refers

to in the subtitle should be credited with reopening a debate on this issue in the field of architecture and acquiring a certain degree of popularity. It then spread and triggered further studies and researches that confirmed the return of *post-operaismo* in the early twenty-first century, i.e., of a perspective which, as in the sixties, considered production as the battleground between capital and antagonist forces—in my opinion correctly identifying the risk of becoming "a cultured reference for a tired academy".

21 The discussion in Milan in the seventies, launched by Alberto Magnaghi, Cesare Stevan, Augusto Perelli, and other teachers at the Faculty of Architecture, was based on the theoretical positions of the "*Città Fabbrica*" and illustrated the magazine *Quaderni del territorio*; it considered "corporate and productive totality" as the subjugation of the city to capital.

22 *Contropiano*, for example, was the most interdisciplinary of the workers' magazines from 1968–71, founded by Alberto Asor Rosa, Massimo Cacciari, and Antonio Negri. Authors included Manfredo Tafuri, Francesco Dal Co, Marco De Michelis, and Massimo Cacciari. In 1968, the year *Contropiano* was founded, Manfredo Tafuri was invited to Venice by Giuseppe Samonà. In 1969, he published the article entitled "*Per una critica dell'ideologia architettonica*", a topic he took up again in 1973, in *Progetto e Utopia. Architettura e sviluppo capitalistico*, Bari: Laterza, 1973 (*Architecture and Utopia: Design and Capitalist Development*, Cambridge: MIT Press, Cambridge, 1976). There were also *Quaderni del territorio* and *Città Classe*, magazines of the two juxtaposed positions of the Milanese group of the *Città Fabbrica* and the Venetian group of the *Città del capitale* or the *Uso capitalistico del territorio*.

23 The occupation of the faculty of architecture in Milan should be seriously reviewed; it involved occupation, the suspension of teachers, and the assumption of responsibilities by an excellent dean, Carlo De Carli. See: *La Facoltà di Architettura del Politecnico di Milano. 1963–1974. La rivoluzione culturale*, privately printed, 2009 http://www.gizmoweb.org/wp-content/uploads/2009/12/la-rivoluzione-culturale-catalogo-bassa-protetto

24 *Quaderni Piacentini,* 7–8 February 1963, citation in Alfonso Berardinelli, *Casi critici*, Macerata: Quodlibet, 2007: 258

25 It's almost a legend: Panzieri resigned his executive positions at the PSI (the Italian Socialist Party) and moved to Turin in 1959, where he took a job as director of a social sciences series for Einaudi. He launched an independent study with a group of dissidents of the socialist and communist left; the study focused on the conditions of the working class. They revived the fourth section of Book One of *Das Kapital* and of the "Fragment on Machines" of the *Grundrisse*, in trying to apply Marx's ideas of formal subsumption and real subsumption of the labour process to capital to the analysis of the transformations of factories. The *Quaderni Rossi* group was formed and publication began in 1961.

26 Antonio Negri and Michael Hardt, *Empire*, Cambridge: Harvard University Press, 2000; *Multitude: War and Democracy in the Age of Empire*, New York: Penguin, 2004

27 Negri's theory of insubordination is an important part of the structure of workerism in the seventies. He was the head of the faction that, reviewing Lenin's theory, founded *Potere Operaio* in 1969. This faction opposed the positions assumed by Tronti, Cacciari, and Asor Rosa, who theorised a shift of the conflict into the state/public domain.

28 Luc Boltanski and Arnaud Esquerre, *Enrichment: A Critique of Commodities*, Cambridge: Polity Press, 2020

29 Cristina Corradi, "Panzieri, Tronti, Negri: le diverse eredità dell'operaismo italiano", in Pier Paolo Poggio (eds.), *L'altronovecento. Comunismo eretico e pensiero critico, vol. II, Il sistema e i movimenti - Europa 1945–1989*, Milano: Fondazione L. Micheletti - Jaca Book, 2011: 223–247. Undoubtedly the international success of the last books by Negri and Hardt sparked many reinterpretations of Italian *operaismo*.

30 A discussion about the mass certainly

cannot be contained in a note. The mass is the twentieth-century form of the emancipated body: "a powerful body" (Sigmund Freud, *Mass Psychology and Other Writings*, New York: Penguin, 2004 – first ed. 1921); an "enigma" (Elias Canetti, *Crowds and Power*, New York: Farrar Straus & Giroux, 1984). In the mass the body becomes serial; it is between and with other bodies. Canetti considers the mass as gravitation and attraction, as something that gives symbolic and political form to power. It can kill and attract. Mass is first and foremost the endless mass of the dead, of bodies that no longer exist. It is fire, wheat, forest, rain, sand, wind, sea, and money. It is the "psychic scene" of the schizophrenic. It has a physical, corporeal dimension. It is the construction of a single collective corpus. Through its liturgies, it becomes populace. And this is already very clear in early twentieth-century German culture, something Giorgio Agamben explains in *Il regno e la gloria. Per una genealogia teologica dell'economia e del governo*, Milano: Neri Pozza, 2007. Throughout the twentieth century, architecture has become, in different ways, the theatre of the body of mass.

31 Negri is an attentive scholar of Spinoza. He wrote *The Savage Anomaly: The Power of Spinoza's Metaphysics and Politics*, Minneapolis: University of Minnesota Press, 1991, and *Subversive Spinoza*, Manchester: Manchester University Press, 2004. The link is also debated in Vicente Serrano, *La herida de Spinoza. Felicidad y política en la vida postmoderna*, Barcelona: Anagrama, 2011. Without this premise, perhaps, one can understand little of the concept of *Multitude*. Negri considers Spinoza's work as outlining a revolutionary project. He attributes to Spinoza the idea that being always means being subversively part of the *Multitude*. More precisely, Negri re-elaborates Spinoza through Deleuze, combining Spinoza's concept of power with the Marxist theory of productive force (and supports Corradi, "Panzieri, Tronti, Negri: le diverse eredità dell'operaismo

italiano", cit., with Nietzsche's concept of desire for power to create a bridge between ontology and politics). "Denying dualism between soul and body, hierarchies of the being and orders dedicated to action, the Dutch philosopher enables, according to Negri, identification of a modern materialist tradition, alternative to the dialectical tradition, and centred on the constitutive process of desire". Ivi

32 Antonio Negri, *Arte e Moltitudo*, Roma: DeriveApprodi, 2014; the book contains the letters written in the late eighties. The one I refer to is entitled "About the body", p. 77

33 Ivi: 77–78 (underlining by the author).

34 Ivi.: 110

35 I refer, for example, to Étienne Balibar, Sandro Mezzadra, and, for some issues, to Slavoj Žižek, Alain Badiou, David Harvey and, as a feminist, to Alisa Del Re.

36 For example, those pertaining to the Lefebvrian social construction of space. Henri Lefebvre, *The Production of Space*, Oxford: Blackwell, 1991

37 Judith Butler and Athena Athanasiou, *Dispossession: The Performative in the Political*, Malden: Polity Press, 2013

38 Judith Butler, *Notes Toward a Performative Theory of Assembly*, Cambridge: Harvard University Press, 2015. The book was written in 2015, before Trump was elected, at a time when the movements that for a decade had taken place in the streets were still in people's minds: the Occupy movement, the protests in Athens, the so-called "Arab Spring", Gezi Park in Istanbul, queer mobilisation, and mobilisation by irregular immigrants. There was an increase in movements of dissent towards neoliberal logic and against repressive governments and powers. These movements were continuously referred to. For more on this issue, see: Butler and Athanasiou, *Dispossession: The Performative in the Political*, cit. "What is the political significance of assembling as bodies, stopping traffic or claiming attention, or moving not as stray and separated individuals, but as social movement of some kind? …. The "We are here" that translates that collective

bodily presence might be re-read as "We are *still* here" meaning "We have not yet been disposed of. We have not slipped quietly into the shadows of public life: we have not become the glaring absence that structures your public life", p. 196

39 Butler, *Notes Toward a Performative Theory of Assembly*, cit.: 236–237 (in the Italian translation).

40 This issue was tackled, for example, by Pier Luigi Crosta, *La produzione sociale del piano*, Milano: Franco Angeli, 1983; *La politica del piano*, Milano: Franco Angeli, 1989; *Politiche. Quale conoscenza per l'azione*, Milano: Franco Angeli, 1998; Gabriele Pasqui, *Città popolazioni politiche*, Milano: Jaca Book, 2008; *Urbanistica oggi. Piccolo lessico critico*, Roma: Donzelli, 2017; Cristina Bianchetti, *Urbanistica e sfera pubblica*, Roma: Donzelli, 2008; *Il Novecento è davvero finito*, Roma: Donzelli, 2011; *Spazi che contano*, Roma: Donzelli, 2016

41 Hannah Arendt, *The Human Condition*, Chicago: University of Chicago Press, 1958: 198–199

42 Since their radical differences are not the focus of the considerations in this book, I shall deal with them rapidly in this note. I refer to the divergence of the regulating idea of public sphere/space, such as Habermas' communicative action, in which one fights and conquers consensus; Arendt's idea insists on the plurality of needs and visions that, even in this case, find some form of reconciliation; the idea of public space as a battleground where different hegemonic projects are compared without the possibility of reconciliation because an oppositive identity is re-articulated when, as Mouffe states, counter-hegemonic politics succeeds in disarticulating existing power relations. See *Sul politico*, Milano: Bruno Mondadori, 2007; Id., *Il conflitto democratico*, Milano: Mimesis, 2015

43 Judith Butler, *Gender Trouble: Feminism and the Subversion of Identity*, London: Routledge, 1990

44 Butler and Athanasiou, *Dispossession: The Performative in the Political*, cit.

45 Esposito's passage about biological life as the object of power recalls a brief observation I shall cite here in note. It involves urban planning literature, which has focused on biopolitics for quite some time.
Many considerations have been made of the city, starting with the essay by Jacques Dreyfus, *La città disciplinare. Saggio sull'urbanistica*, Milano: Feltrinelli, 1978, and more recently but still some time ago, the issue of the magazine *Millepiani* focusing on *Biopolitics and territory*, no. 9 (1996). Roughly ten years later came Andrea Cavalletti, *La città biopolitica. Mitologie della sicurezza*, Milano: Bruno Mondadori, 2005 and the review by Sernini for *L'Indice* (January 2006) mentioning Sennett's (less well-known) book, *Flesh and Stone. The Body and the City in Western Civilization*, London: Faber & Faber, 1994. In a note in the Introduction (Michele Sernini recalls), Sennett admits that he began to study the body fifteen years earlier with his friend Foucault. When Foucault died, Sennett stopped working on it. He picked the topic up again years later in a way that would not have curried favour with the young Foucault, but was inspired by the last years of Foucault's life—when "he had lost the paranoia about control that had marked part of his life" and, prior to his death, had become more interested in people and individuals. In my opinion these ideas are crossroads in an interesting collective discussion; we could perhaps point out that they focus on topics such as the police and safety, rather than the way in which the latter not only creep into the intensity and variability of relations and social relationships but also into the way in which they design space.

46 See, for example, the extensive collected volume (of almost 600 pages) coordinated by Deborah Hauptmann, entitled *Cognitive Architecture. From Biopolitics to NooPolitics. Architecture and Mind in the Age of Communication and Information*, Rotterdam: 010Publishers, 2010

47 Roberto Esposito, "La rivincita della carne", *L'Espresso*, (27 August 2017), 29–31

48 Ivi

DISPOSSESSION

*The important thing about
housing is not what it is,
but what is does in people's lives.*
Turner, 1976[1]

"If You Can Build a House
Between Sunset and Sunrise..."[2]

In 1976 John Turner returned to England from America, where in the
early seventies he had worked with Donald Schön on an assessment of self-
construction in the United States. That year, he published the book *Housing
by People*[3] as part of the non-academic, radical series entitled *Ideas in Progress*.
The goal of the series was to highlight "alternatives to industrial society".[4]
In his preface, Colin Ward painted a sort of family portrait of John Turner,
Giancarlo de Carlo, Pat Crooke, and himself in Venice in 1952, discussing
"who provides and who decides in housing and planning".[5] Their close relationship with the anarchist magazine *Freedom* (founded by Peter Kropotkin)
and the leaflet *Volontà* (directed by Giancarlo de Carlo) had brought them
all together some time earlier.[6]

John Turner was a graduate of the Architectural Association School of Architecture, and during his studies he spent a year on secondment with the BBPR
partnership in Italy. This is not why he became famous. His fame was due
to the positions he developed during his nine long years in Peru and later in
Cambridge, Massachusetts. He spent another eight years at the Joint Center for Urban Studies at MIT and at the department of Urban Studies and
Planning at Harvard University, where he cultivated a solid critical position
against the rationality of mass housing policies for the poor, which despite
the enormous resources that were made available never achieved their goals.
What's more, they never questioned their goals, merely assumed them as
natural; their (only) dilemma was how to improve their ability to achieve
these goals without trying to critically assess them. *Houses for the poor* is a
paradoxical policy that rationally pursues goals with a doubtful rationality;

ones that are presented as natural social development laws. By contrast, the informal and unofficial nature of cities "built by poverty" offers a slim chance to limit the conditions of intolerable precarity through social support networks and information and decentralising technologies[7]—in other words, thanks to their ability to create new situations or mobilise a certain number of effects. This is the key idea in *Housing by People*. Referring to Turner means rediscovering the matrices of an idea that persists in the international debate, one that considers occupants' autonomy the solution to their problem. The debate could go on and on.

The "housing problem" became a key topic in the political debate in Italy more or less at the same time as the publication of *Housing by People*. In 1972, Francesco Indovina wrote about the problem in *Lo spreco edilizio*, a collected volume that carried a certain weight.[8] There were several reasons for its importance: clearly, the deterioration of housing conditions, but also the political debate about reform initiatives, the materialisation of a specific conflict, the goal of unions to turn housing into a social service, and the crisis of the building sector. Dwelling became the testing ground where many ideas about the relationship between technical culture and society were called into question. Extensive material "was stacked and shifted from tables and chairs".[9]

As far as I know, no explicit references to Max Weber were made during this debate; however, the focus was on the regulatory-institutional matrix as a factor explaining how society is held together. A far cry from the autonomy demanded by John Turner. This is one way of interpreting the great battle against urban rent[10]—although it can also be interpreted ethically and religiously, based on the contents of the pastoral letter by the abbot Giovanni Franzoni, who was suspended from his position after the letter was published.[11] Norms, provisions, and laws concerning the housing problem were examined in order to query how society tries to self-regulate by dealing with its more radical problems. Some believed the tension between regulations and society was the most advantageous viewpoint from which to search for virtuous changes in regulations. Others used references to laws defensively. The season during which the Housing Question was considered the hub of a social regulation model that slowly became irretrievably flawed remains one of the most far-reaching architectural and urban planning debates in Italy. The long postwar period had come to an end.

So, what remains of the seventies' debate? Precisely what Turner had in mind, and is now at the centre of the international debate: the problem of hovels, shacks, and houses that aren't houses but shelters, retreats, or refuges. Uninhabitable houses. A Poverty Commission was set up in Italy after the war; its task was to assess both the living conditions of the poor and the performance of social welfare institutions. On 12 October 1951, the Italian Parliament voted in favour of the bill establishing the Commission. The social democrat Ezio Vigorelli became its chair, while the film director Giorgio Ferroni was asked to produce a documentary on the issue for the Istituto Luce.[12] Ferroni was a good documentary filmmaker; he put together what we would now call a modern inquiry, based on the Commission documents, to tell the story of the people and places affected. At the time, this meant outlining the modernity of working families and the backwardness of the rural community. That was where hovels could be found.[13] Following this, the "rising tide that lifts all boats" shifted the problem of uninhabitable houses to that of middle-class housing. The problem of hovels seemed to be relegated to a past that was to be forgotten. Other issues regarding housing were raised.[14]

It is only in the last twenty years that the problem of uninhabitable houses, now included in the concept of *radical housing*,[15] has once again become a key issue. Scholars and activists are mobilised in the fight for the right to housing almost everywhere in the geographical invention known as Global South. A radical approach is inseparable from attention to everyday practices. The phenomenology is widespread, and includes dwellings in precarious, hidden places, in shelters, refuges, and camps; that is, uninhabitable homes everywhere. And the numbers are staggering: according to UN-Habitat, there were 1.6 billion unsuitable houses in 2014.[16] And the number is growing. It is an unequivocal sign that inequality and precarity are slowly shaping the character of cities.[17]

Turner's positions are part of this revival because they query what (this kind of) housing can do for its occupants. Turner is generally relocated in a Marxist-heretical or decidedly anarchist perspective, one which states that housing is a right: a right to have a shelter, to occupy, and to resist eviction and violent removal. It's not very different from Colin Ward's acquired right to "build a house between sunset and sunrise". It's as if we've gone back to basics: housing is no longer a space (a house) provided by the state, self-constructed, conquered, or inherited; nor the recreation of one's own Arcadia;[18] nor is there a repositioning oneself as an owner, since ownership conveys the idea that we are owners of our own person. Instead, the old Housing Question—in terms of the privation of a fundamental right—is supported by a principle of justice. Better still, by a *moral economy* like the one characterising the struggles for bread studied by Edward Thompson.[19] A nineteenth-and-twentieth-century approach (and, according to Thompson, one even older than that). I have discussed this issue in relation to the deflagration of the concept of urban rights within neo-liberalist policies.[20] I would now like to pursue a different position with dispossession as its core issue. The hope is that this concept will make it possible to question the spaces of *radical housing*, just like *mētis* questioned those of individual and scattered dwelling in the nineties.[21]

Dispossession

The genealogy of the concept of dispossession has numerous ramifications. The concept was introduced by Erving Goffman in his studies in the late fifties and early sixties in the context of people in asylums.[22] Goffman introduces *dispossession* as the expropriation of the subject implemented through material and corporeal procedures: taking their photograph, weighing them, taking their fingerprints, assigning them a number, and listing their personal belongings before taking them into custody, undressing, washing, and disinfecting them, cutting their hair, giving them institutional clothes, telling them about the rules, and assigning them places. These procedures separate people from the world; they introduce a body into an administrative machine so that their actions, and maybe even their character, can be programmed and moulded.

When the term *dispossession* appeared, it was used to refer to colonial logic, expropriations, and withdrawal of land—but also to eviction and expulsion, the dispossession of a sphere of intimacy, of a private domain, of a right. It is the literal meaning of the term that prevails: placing someone outside the domain of property; to expel, to exile, to abandon.

Feminist literature much later introduces the term with a double meaning.[23] As a reflective form of self-subjection: "we are dispossessed of ourselves by virtue of some kind of contact with another, by virtue of being moved and even surprised or disconcerted by that encounter with alterity".[24] One is moved towards the other and by the other. In this initial variant, it seems to me that there is a revival (but in reverse) of Lacan's concept of *extimité*, which is redefined here as self-dislocation. In *extimité* we bring part of ourselves to the surface; it is a movement from the intimate to the extimate. Both terms represent the different and differential manner in which the anxieties and the excitements of relationality are socially distributed.[25] Mourning, pain, love, anger, and ecstasy empty us; it is a process of draining and exposure vis-à-vis others that underlines the social-passionate character of the person and the anxieties and emotions of practices. This is the first form of dispossession. The second is a coercive form, one in which dispossession is endured: we depend on those powers "that alternately sustain or deprive us".[26] In this case, dispossession is the expression of a paternalistic and authoritarian system of control. It refers to processes and ideologies that expropriate and eject people using normative and normalising powers: the dark side of the regulation that keeps society together. This form of dispossession is "mapped onto our bodies through normative matrices but also through situated practices of raciality, gender, sexuality, intimacy, able-bodiedness, economy and citizenship."[27] In both senses, dispossession involves the subject's relations to norms.

The concept of dispossession can be used to describe the relationship between the body and space in the dimension of power. And this helps us to move (sideways, but perhaps also forward) the traditional way of dealing with the problem of uninhabitable houses, which is still flawed by excessive generalisation. As it is based on the privation of or demand for a right, it strips the issue back to its minimum; a similar approach is adopted in different economic and social contexts, such as refugee camps in Turkey and Greece, slums in Laos and Lima, and uninhabitable houses in Cambodia and Mexico City. By contrast, dispossession is intimately associated with specific conditions, embedded in bodies and places. It admits no generalisations. To discuss this concept I have tried to use it to describe one of the many common forms of *radical housing* in contemporary cities: an authorised camp or rest area for the Romani people in Turin.[28]

Dwelling in the Camp

The camp in Via Germagnano (Turin) was opened in 2004 to provide housing for Romani families who had been violently removed from other places in the city.[29] It is an equipped rest area: a project very similar to a decidedly elementary concept of a low-density neighbourhood with little houses, pathways, and *piazzuole* (lay-bys/small squares). Thirty little houses are occupied by 129 individuals—although only sixty-three were actually authorised to reside in this area. The three unauthorised areas next to the equipped area, on the other hand, are occupied by a far higher number of individuals (391).[30] Half of the population are women who play an important role in the management of extended family groups. A total of 520 individuals, who have radically modified spaces and houses in both the small authorised settlement and the three adjacent, self-built areas, joined and separated by rather thick vegetation, debris, and waste.[31] The camp is located on the shores of the river Stura, roughly five kilometres from the city centre, in an area with superimposed infrastructure belts and big productive settlements. The invariable and unachieved objective of local administrative policies was to clean up the camp.

As in other, similar cases, the precarity of the camp is not due to forms of unsettled, community, or nomadic housing, but rather to exposure to demolitions, evictions, the sometimes-difficult interactions between those who live there, and harmful environmental conditions. Dealing with these cases is complicated, and it isn't easy to avoid humanist dramaturgy veined with paternalism. When the weight of the social world becomes this heavy, it is easy to slip into compassionate conservatism.[32]

A Roma woman (37) from Bosnia with three children was one of the first to be assigned a house in Via Germagnano. Among the other inhabitants: an old Khorakhane Muslim (80), the head of the largest extended family in the camp, who describes himself by listing his descendants—six children, who each have six, seven, nine, or twelve children. He recalls that they were peasants in Travnik, Bosnia; that they owned land and cultivated potatoes, beans, and corn; that they bred horses, but were continuously evicted by the army, until one day they decided to move to Italy, where they became tinkers and scrap dealers: "nomads by necessity".[33] A young woman (21) who tried to leave the camp after she lost her job precisely because she lived there. A younger woman (18) who was also looking for work. A woman (31), originally from Bosnia, whose parents from Mostar emigrated when they were very young; she has twelve siblings, each with half a dozen children, and is here in the camp after being evicted from a council house where some of them had lived for fourteen years. A Daxikhané craftsman (65) from Serbia, registered with the Chamber of Commerce, who makes boilers and repairs pipes for heating systems; he has a family of fourteen and is proud to be able to transmit his skills to his sons. Another girl (18) is part of a family of five. Their father comes from Montenegro; she was born in Italy (as were her siblings), attended high school, and is very different to previous generations: her mother still doesn't speak Italian and can't work because she wouldn't know how to get to her place of work. One couple, married for forty years, have Bosnian roots, but don't speak Bosnian. Born in Italy, nomadism is part of their past; their grandparents and fathers are buried here. The sixteen interviews that were part of the survey focused on dwelling practices in the camp in Via Germagnano, highlighting not only where all the occupants came from, but also their expectations and desires, as well as the difficulties associated with living in the camp.

In the interviews, there was constant reference to bodies and their vulnerability. The bodies of the animals that interviewees breed or ward off. The bodies of the children playing outside; they talked about solving the problems of getting to school, sleeping in caravans, and sometimes falling ill. The adult bodies of men and women tackling what they call "the structure of living".[34] This phrase reflects their awareness that dwelling is incarnate in the body and skin and not positioned within a defined spatial order: the little council house, the self-built house, the caravan parked nearby. Bodies have to be sheltered from environmental conditions, from illnesses and social insecurity—tasks that older women tackle by developing strategies, expectations, and proposals. It is crystal-clear that dwelling takes place literally in the encumbrance of the body, as there is not enough space for bodies and dwelling involves continuous spatial adjustments: rooms added or enlarged, new openings, verandas, or even caravans and trucks used as extra rooms[35] turn the house into a disjointed space. The space in the little houses in the rest area is too small for families of twelve or fourteen individuals. Its fixed partitions reflect a completely abstract housing concept. This is visible in the incessant transformations, in the use of outdoor areas, in the degree of neglect that, not unsurprisingly, is less obvious in the three unofficial camps with self-built houses. In other words, the space of dwelling is rigid and brittle when it collides with bodies. It yields to transformative actions, accepts waste, redefines its borders, demolishes fencing and inhabitable spaces, empties itself, and fills itself with the material fragments of the intense recycling of absolutely anything. It is a hard but not crystallised space that accepts dense forms of dwelling created by relational strategies, informal economies, ritual practices, and the affirmation of the extended family unit in exposed environments[36]—and by a certain pride.[37]

Dwelling is never contained in the material-physical form of its space, and much less in the form of the camp. It is more of a generative process: it doesn't maintain things as they are, but reciprocally adapts them. Reciprocal adaptation is also imposed on space; on individuals and families. The relationships between occupying space and the space one occupies structure people's moral conception: their self-belonging, ability to act, and personal identity. It is not always a conciliatory, constructive, calm, virtuous, and improved reciprocal adaptation. Sometimes it is violent, sexist, and conflictual. In the camp, between camps, and, in a dormant but no less radical manner, with the inhabitants of the city.[38]

Happy, anxious, despised human bodies and animals live in and reciprocally adapt space. They adapt their own moral, political, and affective world; sometimes by opening up (as stated by Butler), sometimes by enduring a paternalistic and authoritarian system of control. We should remember that living in a camp means being exposed to the threat of spaces, as well as social ties and one's own integrity, being uprooted and destroyed.[39]

Necessity and Evidence[40]

The interlacement of bodies and space is so intimate that it penetrates and remodels both. Dispossession comes into play when defining this interlacement. Let's go back to Butler: dispossession is the expression of "that which alternately sustain or deprive us".[41] It is an authoritarian force that deprives, that expresses processes of subjection. But at the same time, it supports. The negative, oppressive version of power is crystal-clear: expulsion, privation, removal. But dispossession does not lie in this subjection. We cannot comprehend this approach without references to Foucault's theory of power.[42] Power is not only "a force that says no":[43] it does not translate only into constriction, surveillance, control, and oppression. There is a "productive dimension of power that produces and traverses things, induces pleasure, forms knowledge, produces discourses. A productive network that runs through the whole social body, much more than as a negative instance".[44] Thus the focus is on the manner of this shift—whether we call it the economy or the microphysics of power.[45] Dispossession introduces this complex dimension into the physical dynamics between spaces and bodies.

How? By acting within the complex regulatory matrix that works to produce the appearance of substance. Some matrices are felt to be very remote and foreign, almost incomprehensible, and yet also incumbent and unavoidable: they are the norms regulating affiliation to a status that provides temporary sojourn to those who are stateless. They are a framework of ordinances, police decrees, permits, bureaucratic modules, appeals, and legislative conformity. Other norms are felt to be less remote because they are functional:

these are the administrative and urban planning regulations governing what can or cannot be done in camps with regard to mobility, access to health, education, and safety services.[46] Regulations that are also linked to surveillance and control. Others are intimate and personal: these are the norms governing affiliation to a cultural, linguistic, and behavioural history, no less binding and harsher even than the previous ones as they create forms of dominion over families. They are not just restrictions and prohibitions: they involve communicative structurisation, significance, and knowledge. They all retain a complicated position vis-à-vis corporeal materiality.[47]

Space is almost always the target of all these numerous prescriptions; a space that is never naked. It is imbued with meanings that are fragmented, deflagrated, and multiplied by the regulatory frameworks. Dispossession is these regulatory matrices at work, along with all their regulatory ambivalence that oppresses and supports. "Our father had built a big living room for parties, weddings, funerals, but they demolished it because the camp regulation forbade construction".[48] Threatening space means threatening and questioning the people who live there, people who are different, who have a different sexual orientation, who are different in age.[49] Dispossession generates a very complex psychic, affective, and political effect on bodies. It also affects affectivity and the potential to act and have relationships. It has an effect on the way in which we are there for one another, on the way in which we are exposed to one another. In other words, it feeds into the materialisation and dematerialisation of individuals.[50]

Dispossession highlights not only the vulnerability and precarity of bodies, but also their perseverance and resistance. It forces certain choices or denies others. As mentioned in the interviews, it denies culture, work, house, and time, as well as enforcing the impossibility of avoiding degraded living conditions.[51] It is the visible expression of power dynamics, jointly involving bodies, spaces, and power.

Precarious Exercises

Uninhabitable houses *are still here,* in the shadow of the public life of the city marked by financial capital. They signal the evacuation and dislocation of the fundamental categories of housing and its design: rights, democracy, and citizenship. Categories that are rewritten in cases like those mentioned here, in a context of precarity, and are sometimes shaped by actions that try to solve it, even if those actions are not backed by laws, by cultural, political, and discursive conditions, and by organisational models. Exercises that are, in themselves, precarious. The ongoing presence of uninhabitable houses questions how effective these exercises are. In other words, which operations can be ascribed to design in dispossession situations? Apart from administrative procedures that diminish the complex, opaque, and ambivalent nature of codes and protocols, can inhabitability, affective economics, acknowledgement, non-destructive psychic dynamics, and relational worlds exist in a situation of dispossession? What game are we playing if, as architects and urban planners, we use our epistemic and ontological regimes to act on the processes of precarity and exhaustion intrinsic in dispossession? How is the project structured, approved, and limited by precarity? Or, in more simple terms, to what extent does the design idea fall apart when dealing with that *I am still here* produced and expressed by precarity, by the part of the population left surrounded by poverty, and uncertainty, occupation, and unemployment in these areas, consigning it to what Butler and Athanasiou call "a damaged sense of future"?[52] We need to understand the responsibility of design as an activity that functions within precarity, that is structured, approved, and limited by precarity: in short, as Turner's theory developed in Peru in the sixties does. It also requires us to learn the lesson of feminist theory that merges performativity and precarity and considers dispossession as the source of our reactivity and responsibility towards others.

99

Notes

1   John F. C. Turner, *Housing by People. Towards autonomy in building environments*, London-New York: Marion Boyars, 1976: 5

2   "There is a belief around the world that if you can build a house between sunset and sunrise, then the owner of the land cannot evict you. There are many variations on this theme. The condition might be that the roof is in place, or that a pot is boiling on the fire, or that smoke can be seen emerging from the chimney". Colin Ward, *Cotters and Squatters: Housing's Hidden History*, Nottingham: Free Leaves, 2002: 5

3   Turner, *Housing by People. Towards autonomy in building environments*, cit.

4   Ivan Illich and Rosalyn Lindheim, amongst others, had already published in *Ideas in Progress*.

5   Turner, *Housing by People. Towards autonomy in building environments*, cit.: 10

6   Giancarlo de Carlo considered the book by John Turner and Robert Fichter, *Freedom to Build*, London: Macmillan, 1972, as a possible publication for the *Il Saggiatore* series he directed. See: Corinna Nicosia, *L'Ilses oltre l'Ilses. Un esperimento riformista (mancato) e le sue eredità culturali*, PhD diss., Politecnico di Milano, Academic Year 2015–2016

7   Turner, *Housing by People. Towards autonomy in building environments*, cit.: 13–14 "Good housing like plentiful food is more common where it is locally produced through network structures

and decentralizing technologies. The thesis in this book is that these are the only ways and means through which satisfactory goods and services can be obtained, and that they are vital for a stable planet".

8 Francesco Indovina (ed.), *Lo spreco edilizio*, Padova: Marsilio, 1972: VII

9 Ivi: VII

10 Fiorentino Sullo, *Lo scandalo urbanistico. Mezzo secolo*, Firenze: Vallecchi, 1964. The book is a collection of articles published in *Politica*, the Florentine periodical of the left wing of the Christian Democrat Party, together with the Parliamentary acts and various key documents that accompanied the genesis and controversy around the Sullo Law.

11 Giovanni Franzoni, *La terra è di Dio. Lettera pastorale*, COM Nuovi Tempi, 1973

12 For more information, see: https://luceperladidattica.com/2016/10/24/linchiesta-parlamentare-sulla-miseria-e-su-i-mezzi-per-combatterla-1951-1954-incontro-di-studio-allarchivio-storico-della-camera-dei-deputati/

13 Cristina Bianchetti, *La questione abitativa. Processi politici e attività rappresentative*, Milano: Franco Angeli, 1985

14 Alessandro Pizzorno, "I ceti medi nei meccanismi del consenso", in Fabio L. Cavazza and Stephen R. Graubard (eds.), *Il caso italiano*, Milano: Garzanti, 2 Vols, 1974: 315–338

15 Michele Lancione: "Radical housing: On the politics of dwelling as difference", *International Journal of Housing Policy*, (2019), DOI: 10.1080/19491247.2019.1611121

16 Cit. in Michele Lancione, "Radical housing: On the politics of dwelling as difference", cit.: 1; UN-Habitat, *Forced evictions*, Fact Sheet No. 25/Rev.1 (2014). Retrieved from https://www.ohchr.org/Documents/Publications/FS25.Rev.1.pdf; UN-Habitat, *Urbanization and development: Emerging futures. World Cities Report 2016*, Nairobi: United Nations Human Settlements Program, (2016)

17 Secchi had asked the question in 2013: *La città dei ricchi e la città dei poveri*, Bari: Laterza, 2013. Since then there has been an exponential boom in literature on this issue.

18 Dennis Hardy and Colin Ward, *Arcadia for All. The Legacy of a Makeshift Landscape*, Nottingham: Five Leaves, 2004

19 Edward Thompson, *The Moral Economy of the English Crowd in the Eighteenth Century* https://libcom.org/files/MORAL%20ECONOMY%20OF%20THE%20ENGLISH%20CROWD.pdf Italian translation in *Società patrizia. Cultura plebea. Otto saggi di antropologia storica sull'Inghilterra del Settecento*, Torino: Einaudi, 1981: 57–136

20 Cristina Bianchetti, *Spazi che contano*, Roma: Donzelli, 2016; Id., "Il progetto nella pluralizzazione dei diritti", *ARDETH* #4 (2019), 209–222

21 Cristina Bianchetti, *Abitare la città contemporanea*, Milano: Skira, 2003

22 Erving Goffman, *Asylums: Essays on the Social Situation of Mental Patients and Other Inmates*, Harmondsworth: Penguin, 1968 (first ed. 1961)

23 Judith Butler and Athena Athanasiou, *Dispossession: The Performative in the Political*, Malden: Polity Press, 2013: 2

24 Ivi: 3

25 Ivi: 92

26 Ivi: 4

27 Ivi: 18

28 An initial version in Cristina Bianchetti and Matilde Cembalaio, *Cosa fa una casa? Politica, etica ed economia affettiva della spoliazione*, at the meeting *Re-Hab*, Turin, (6 and 7 December 2019). These considerations were inspired by the survey performed in early 2019 by Matilde Cembalaio and reported in *Fuori dai margini. L'abitare formale e informale nell'area di via Germagnano a Torino*, Graduate Th., Politecnico di Torino, September 2019

29 It has a much longer history, as illustrated in Marco Revelli, *Fuori luogo. Cronaca di un campo Rom*, Torino: Bollati Boringhieri, 1999

30 Statistics provided by the Municipal Police, Specialist Unit Service, Informative Unit on Ethnic Minorities of the city of Turin on 17 January 2019. Cembalaio, *Fuori dai margini. L'abitare*

formale e informale nell'area di via Germagnano a Torino, cit.: 54

31 Dividing elements, demolitions, additional rooms, and expedients, as well as the debris that remains after the destruction of several small houses, are accurately identified and described in Cembalaio, *Fuori dai margini. L'abitare formale e informale nell'area di via Germagnano a Torino*, cit.

32 Lauren Berlant, *Compassion: The Culture and Politics of an Emotion*, London: Routledge, 2004: collective articles illustrating a sort of genealogy of the concept of compassion in literature, psychoanalysis, and social history.

33 Cembalaio, *Fuori dai margini. L'abitare formale e informale nell'area di via Germagnano a Torino*, cit.: 289. All the following citations are taken from this graduate thesis.

34 Ivi: 349

35 "These little houses they've given us are 45 square metres … I've enlarged and modified it. I was reported, then I got myself a lawyer, the case was statute-barred and so it remained the way it was". Ivi: 347

36 "A house allows you to be with other people". Ivi: 349

37 "It's nice to be Roma, and know how to muddle through". Ivi: 296

38 "We're called gypsies, when people see us they say go away … but not all gypsies are the same". Ivi: 344–345. "Even if I want to fit in with you Italians there'll always be an Italian who will discriminate against me, or my children, there'll always be someone … I've been fighting against this for 29 years … but it will continue … so I believe that what's important for me is to be with my family, my husband's family, because in the end I don't have any place to go back to". Ivi: 337

39 "They give us a house, they take away the house". Ivi: 285

40 Michel Foucault, *Discipline and Punish: The Birth of the Prison*, London: Penguin, 1981

41 Butler and Athanasiou, *Dispossession: The Performative in the Political*, cit.: 4

42 Judith Butler, *The Psychic Life of Power: Theories in Subjection*, Redwood: Stanford University Press, 1997

43 "What makes power hold good, what makes it accepted, is simply the fact that it doesn't weigh on us as *a force that says no*, that it traverses and produces things, that it induces pleasure, forms knowledge, produces discourses. It needs to be considered as a *productive network* which runs through the whole social body, much more than a negative instance whose function is repression" (italics mine). Michel Foucault, "Interview with Michel Foucault" in *Microfisica del potere. Interventi politici*, Alessandro Fontana and Pasquale Pasquino (eds.), Torino: Einaudi, 1977: 13. Translation from the Italian.

44 *Ibidem*

45 *Ibidem*. With "economy of power", Foucault means "the procedures which allowed the effects of power to circulate in a manner at once continuous, uninterrupted, adopted, and 'individualised' throughout the entire social body". See also *Discipline and Punish: The Birth of the Prison*, cit.

46 "The Municipality has forbidden, for example, you cannot stay here without a permit, but no-one knows why". Cembalaio, *Fuori dai margini. L'abitare formale e informale nell'area di via Germagnano a Torino*, p. 336. "There was a little house, a micro-nest, a space for a billiards hall and a place where children could play … it was working well for a while. When the municipality closed it down we no longer spent time together". Ivi: 249

47 Butler and Athanasiou, *Dispossession: The Performative in the Political*, cit.: 98

48 Cembalaio, *Fuori dai margini. L'abitare formale e informale nell'area di via Germagnano a Torino*, p. 341

49 Living in a camp means being exposed to the threat of the uprooting and destruction of spaces, social ties, one's integrity and dignity. An abrasion of a culture that has developed over a long period of time and is in most cases experienced as trauma and loss, but which also has very material aspects: "If they send me away, I'll have to get a caravan and put it somewhere: where can I go with so many children?" Ivi: 285; "Since day one I wanted to leave

the camp, so did my sister and brother, we tried everything, we want to leave this camp because we're fed up, to take a shower you have to fetch some water, then you have to heat it, then at night if it's cold you get sick and you can't do things, you can't go to school, and regarding wood you first have to chop it". Ivi: 326

50 Dematerialisation is clearly expressed in memories. "Have animals and live like the Romani people: travel with dogs and horses, be free, be stopped from doing something, have a house, live in it with many people". Ivi: 285; "We called them Roma … accustomed to be free", to "be together in the evening, light the fire, chat… we changed and lost our customs because we came here". Ivi: 285

51 "If they give me a council flat, if they give us even a small plot of land, with all my heart, I'll pack and leave because here we live with dogs and cats, we can't breathe easy, our children are always dirty, there's no electricity, water, there's nothing here, I'd like to go out, but where can we go? Out on the street with our families, 20 people in parking areas; the problem is we have nowhere to go". Ivi: 333

52 Butler and Athanasiou, *Dispossession: The Performative in the Political*, cit.: 43

THE PLACE
OF THE BODY.
CONCLUSIONS

Touching the body (or some singular body) with the incorporeality of "sense." And consequently, to make the incorporeal touching, to make of meaning a touch.
Nancy, 2008[1]

Discontinuous and Fractured Parabola

The dawn of the twentieth century began with the *Les demoiselles d'Avignon* by Picasso—five naked women in a brothel—and ended with Bacon's deformed and butchered bodies. Throughout the century, the body was at the centre of tragic events: crowds, masses, armies, bands, gatherings, revolutions, death camps, and ethnic cleansing. For a long time, detachment and moving beyond were common in the field of art. Then, in the late twentieth century, there was an abrupt revival. The painting by Picasso paved the way for the abstract, mental construction of art; Bacon ended that approach with the physical, corporeal logic of sensation. There is no narration; merely the absolute centrality of the body. It is this centrality, exasperated in images of the body in a claustrophobic space of tondi, ovals, and parallelepipeds, that exorcises and removes any narration, conferring tragic materiality on the body. Bacon's bodies do not tell a story: they show that they are flesh. The isomorphism of spiritual torments and deformation: the relationship between body and spirit primarily manifest in suffering. These figures convey the hysterical reality of the body:[2] contractures, paralyses, hyperaesthesia, pressure, dilation, contraction, and crushing. In one of Gilles Deleuze's essays on Bacon, he writes about the problem of capturing forces. He does not directly involve Spinoza, whom he knows well; in 1980 Deleuze dedicated a course at the College de France to Spinoza.[3] But he writes using Spinoza's words. The problem of capturing forces merges with another problem: that of the composition and recomposition of effects. How can invisible forces be made visible through bodies?[4]

Focusing on the body creates discontinuous and fractured trajectories—even in architecture and urbanism, where there are numerous references to the role of the body or the phenomenological imperatives of using our senses "in relearning to look at the world".[5] Nevertheless, these appeals to the body and senses are damaged, discontinuous, and fractured. I have illustrated several fragments in the previous pages of this book. There are undoubtedly many more, but in general it's true that the body is a hidden topic, nestling in the shadows. Urban design has always focused on sick, healthy, happy, and pleasurable bodies. Bodies to be nurtured or to be driven away, hidden, cured. Bodies looked at, scrutinised, caught in the crucible of psychoanalysis, capable of expressing the extraneity of that which is within us. Or removed, absent, obsessed with losses, rejections, omissions, hesitations, dreams; bodies emancipated and insurgent in public space. The project has always focused on bodies, but it has kept them at the outer fringes of its own critical perimeter. So what is the position of the body in urbanism? The question immediately unravels into many others: what are the specific ways in which the design of a city, territory, environment, or landscape considers the body? How does it refer to it? How does it modify, change, shift, and question the body? What does designing mean, if designing is designing the relationship between body and space? Where neither the former nor the latter are simply abstract images, concepts, or roles? In other words, what does it mean to design without functionalism?

Touching the Body

Designing the relationship between body and space means touching the body with design. "Touching the body" is the key theme in Jean-Luc Nancy's ontology: an idea that surfaces in many of his texts, starting with the short but intense philosophical work *Corpus.*[6] Jacques Derrida dedicates a lengthy volume to this emerging idea.[7] Touching means modifying, changing, shifting, questioning what we touch. Design touches the body because, first and foremost, it acts in space. But, in a no less meaningful manner, because it touches the body with sense.

Nancy says of writing that it is "touching the body … with the incorporeal of sense";[8] "to make the incorporeal touching, to make of meaning a sense". He adds: "I won't bother arguing that I'm not praising some dubious 'touching literature.' I know the difference between writing and flowery prose, but *I know of no writing that doesn't touch*".[9] Sense is what allows us to touch. It is a tangible action. Design can be considered (this is my own thought) as a weakly structured ensemble of practices and competences that "touch" the body. It touches the body with the incorporeal of sense and, at the same time, with the corporeal of the changes it generates in the ground and space: in their morphology, their physical infrastructure facilities and their economies. Touching leads to modification, shifting, and calling into question; expressing provisions, values, regulations, and objectives.

Design touches the body with the incorporeal of sense. It does this first by adjectivising it: a body that is sick, healthy, mad. Adjectivisation facilitates, directs, and allows design. It is as if, without qualifying the body (as sick, healthy, mad) there would be a loss of all recognisable forms of the body; it would become a smooth body, "rounded like a soap bubble".[10] An incorporeal body. But then this touching also has an effect. Design touches the body and something is redefined: the ground, facilities, economies, architectures. It touches the body that is troubled by its own obsessions and designs houses with "spider legs" and uterine interiors, promoting a much broader and more blurred idea of environmental, social, and economic protection. It touches the body that enjoys nature to the point of losing itself in it, affected by an outside that boosts its abilities—and this generates the concept of garden, arcadia, and landscape. Design touches the body trapped in mass housing that tries to understand how it can leave an impression of itself. It touches the bodies that are "foreign although they are in the centre",[11] and reconsiders porosity and the many ways in which space is public. It touches the bodies of counterculture, dilated and enhanced by faith in the community and in one's own rebellion, and it considers the neoliberal city as a shimmering device that has gluttonously sucked up its values. It touches the *Multitude* of bodies that live in the global market, endure its inequalities, are expropriated from their jobs and their lives, and see the *everywhere* of their condition in the contemporary city: the concrete, physical, spatial forms of inequality.

It touches the liberated bodies of feminist literature, the demand for a liveable life in precarity and vulnerability, and finds itself rethinking the space in which it becomes visible to others. It is, however, not as consequential, determined, and univocal as it may seem from these hasty references. Above all, it is not a tribute to what Jean-Luc Nancy calls an equally dubious "touching urbanism". It's a different way of looking at things. There are at least two aspects of this different way of looking at things that need to be emphasised. The first involves the intensity of touch; the second the fragility and resistance of the body.

The *intensity of touch*. There is a graduation, a transformation, of touch. As Derrida himself writes, there are many nuances between a caress and a blow.[12] At one extreme, the light, enriching touch, revealing the universe open to the body; or a touching-without-touching that alludes, reveals, enriches. Little more is needed. At the other extreme, the reversal of everything; the construction of a "new body" that destroys everything that went before, a concept tragically echoed in Artaud's words:

"Who am I? / Where do I come from? / I am Antonin Artaud / and I say it / as I know to say it / right now/ you will see my existing body / fall apart / and pick itself up / in 10,000 aspects / well-known / a new body / in which you will / never / be able to forget me again".[13]

A blow that leaves one breathless, that transforms the body, makes it fall apart, decomposing and recomposing it "in 10,000 aspects", in the repudiation of every dualism, every monism, every phenomenology, order, and composure. And are not Bacon's actions merely a similar operation?

The intensity of touch was a key issue in art; and also in politics, until it achieved the annulment of the body and the enchainment of power and the body.[14] Enchainment is the expression of a model we have grown used to calling biopolitical; of a naked life where the being of the body is nothing other than the technically organisable modes of one's existence. Enchainment, loss of freedom, self-determination, and dispossession are extreme forms of touch, of dominion over the body, something that was typical of spatial, territorial, and urban policies. There are varying degrees of gradation between enchainment and the light touch that grazes; they all refer to the many ways in which design and its norms touch the body. Relationships of resistance, strength, fatigue, vulnerability, and dispossession. Bodies are measured through the norms of profit, accumulation, verifiability, and debt. What is at stake here is a "powerful resonance"[15] between the body and the design that touches it. The intensity of touch is not only lightness, enrichment, touching without touching, the aperture of sense, but also resonance with a system of social norms, the ability to resist, to become enriched, to acquire force or to be dispossessed and enchained. However, if the "touching" action of design can either free or subjugate, then this exercise involves political responsibility.

The *fragility of the body*. One might object that the body is too fragile to be able to create such a crucial relationship with design. Quite apart from its continuous, Spinoza-like transformations; from the strength it gains or loses; from the pride of those who maintain "bodies that matter"; from new technological hybrids; from resonance with its system of norms; and even from Nancy's radical position in which "bodies are existence, the very act of existence, *being*"[16] … Quite apart from all this (and perhaps in opposition to all this), the body is fragile; it leaves faint stamps. Projects, desires, doubts, dreams, insults, and words are lost. Very little remains of each body. The great utopian ideas of the past were developed to tackle this fragility and avoid the elimination of bodies. "What is a mummy, after all?" Foucault asks himself, if not "the great utopian body that persist throughout time"?[17] Like the golden masks of Mycenaean civilisations: the utopia of the glorious, strong, solar bodies of dead kings. Like funerary paintings and sculptures throughout the years. And like the regular white stone blocks that currently commemorate the dead. Tombs, masks, and stones in which "my body becomes solid like a thing, eternal like a God";[18] utopias to defeat fragility. Because the body is fragile. Its thoughts, gestures, desires, and dreams are quickly lost. Lost are words spoken and listened to; threats and promises unconsidered even by those to whom they were made. Very little leaves an impression, and it's not always clear who is interested in these impressions. The topic of memory and its transmission, so dear to design, is nothing but the expression of this evanescence; of the little that remains of the body.

So, how can design touch such a vulnerable and fleeting body? This is where plural declension comes in (and probably distances us forever from Nancy and Derrida). Touching the body means conquering a broader, more general dimension. Design gives the single, individual body a much broader dimension by dealing with it. Design tells the story that goes beyond the body itself and thereby conquers (for the body, but also for itself) a dimension we could call public—or better still, political.[19] By referring to a body that is individual, but alludes to others that are similar or opposite, design overcomes a conformist idea of what is public in a way that does not disclaim Dewey but moves beyond him. Touching the body, and implementing a simultaneously conjunctive and disjunctive logic of touching: not touching means emphasising the public nature of design. The material finiteness of the body is always an allusion to broader questions, such as those of cultural diversity, sexual preferences, role transgression, changed capacities caused by ageing, subordination, authority, power, and spatial injustice. The *place of the body*, precisely because it is *of the body*, alludes to and renders visible issues involving rights, inequalities, time, and memory and its transmission. Considered thus, the *place of the body* is a political place.

In conclusion: can urbanism be reformulated based on attention to the body? Can the centrality of the *place* be replaced by the *place of the body*? And is this advantageous? What effects would this have on the regulation of the territory, on major urban issues and how we deal with them? I have tried to identify the ways in which direct or indirect forms of relationship between the body, design, and space are established. Ways in which the body has already been the very delicate link between design and the transformations of space. Ways that refer to administrative procedures, to the simplification of codes, to complex dispossession processes, to regulatory frameworks, and to actions that "touch" the body with the incorporeal of sense as well as with the corporeal of the ground and space, their morphologies, physical infrastructural facilities, and economies. In many cases, design culture has tackled carnality, deformation, psychic aspects, and the ability to weave relationships with bodies; it has introduced vulnerability, volubility, and multiplicity, unhinging functionalist approaches and repeatedly raising questions. The *place of the body* is, after all, a metaphor that creates these questions. Or, if you like, design needs to touch the body to touch values: utopias that move beyond the individual body. A long time ago, Robert Louis Stevenson narrated it perfectly in a Gothic story that became a real apologue. Tension towards freedom requires the body; Henry Jekyll literally requires another body. His hand, "professional in shape and size … large, firm, white, and comely" became Edward Hyde's hand: "lean, corded, knuckly, of a dusky pallor". And so too did his height and step, with "insurgent horror … caged in his flesh".[20] Pursuing freedom means involving the body to the bitter end.

Postscriptum

The way in which urban planning and architecture was narrated in Europe in the last quarter of the twentieth century involved the search for some form of partnership between exploratory design and critical reflection. The fact that the latter gradually became a cultural activity, militancy, political affiliation, expression of an ethics of democracy, or a critique of ideology recalls the painful, complicated phase in which architects and urban planners initially called themselves—particularly in Italy—*condotti* and, shortly afterwards, *operaisti*. Emilio Gentile has at long last narrated the *Crocianesimo* of Italian intellectuals. However, it is important to remember that, in the seventies and eighties, this bond (or contrast, or proximity) between design activity and historical-critical activity sustained "*les enseignements de l'italophilie*".[21] Another world.

A world that evaporated well before the end of the twentieth century. In the ensuing profound transformation of our society, which left nothing intact, how did we rewrite (how do we rewrite?) the relationship between the efforts of imaged design and the theoretical and critical settings in urbanism? Between design and theory? Do we perceive new or renewed models of the dialogue between these two fields? And are there really two fields? Is theory still legitimate and autonomous? Does it still have a task to perform? What do we do today when we try, as I have tried throughout this book, to develop a critique not to provide directions for action but to present attempts to fathom its possibilities?

The question may seem naive, nostalgic, and incorrect. Conflict over the work of critics is not new. We should not forget Tafuri's arguments. But it has taken place in other fields too. I think it was Foucault (or Butler citing Foucault) who spoke of critique as an action supervising a space that it does not intend to police and that it is unable to regulate.[22] An action that is not a function of this task of supervision; it has its own statute, its own legitimacy, and cannot be confused with the expertise of councillors and consultants in the context of the increasing privatisation of research. This is precisely the point. Theory remains important and cannot be dismissed as an ideological, decorative, and superfluous activity.

However, this approach is more interesting now than it was in the past. It is a small pebble thrown into the pond of a university that is reinventing itself and reinventing research in an absolutely productivist and competitive manner. It means claiming the right to be "out-of-place" or to get in the way. Theoretical critique is a form of critique that contrasts with the primacy of the economy and competitiveness of the university. In other words, one that contrasts with the reinvigorated incitement towards an economic discourse that presents itself as technocratic therapy and financial management.

I believe that it is therefore necessary to ask the question: what do we do now when we criticise in order to fathom possibilities? Possibilities constrained by the weakness of design, stuck between the vague empiricism of the profession and the trite implementation of increasingly stringent regulatory norms, with the excuse that they provide some form of sustainability, intelligence, and circularity? The fact that there has, in Italy, been an ongoing philosophical and political review of the role of theory lends weight to my reasoning. And, I'd add, to the argument that the body is key, even in this case.

Notes

1 Jean-Luc Nancy, *Corpus*, New York: Fordham University Press, 2008: 11

2 Gilles Deleuze, *Francis Bacon: The Logic of Sensation*, London: Continuum, 2003

3 Gilles Deleuze *Spinoza*, Paris: PUF, 1970 (in Italian). The posthumous collection of lessons held in Vincennes in 1980–1981; Aldo Pardi (ed.), *Lezioni su Spinoza (Cosa può un corpo? Lezioni su Spinoza)*, Verona: Ombre Corte, 2007

4 Deleuze, *Francis Bacon: The Logic of Sensation*, cit.

5 Maurice Merleau-Ponty, *Phenomenology of Perception*, London: Routledge, 2002 (first ed. 1945), cit.: XXIII

6 Nancy, *Corpus*, cit.

7 Jacques Derrida, *On Touching – Jean-Luc Nancy*, Redwood: Stanford University Press, 2005

8 Nancy, *Corpus*, cit.: 11

9 *Ibidem*

10 Michel Foucault, *The Utopian Body*, radio lecture delivered in 1966. Published in *Sensorium*, MIT Press, (2006), 229–234, cit.: 230

11 Jacques Lacan, *The Seminar, Book VII. The Ethics of Psychoanalysis, 1959–1960*, Jacques-Alain Miller (ed.), New York: Norton & Co., 1992, n. pag.

12 Derrida, *On Touching – Jean-Luc Nancy*, cit.

13 Antonin Artaud, "Post-scriptum, Le Théâtre de la cruauté", in *Œuvres complètes*, Vol. XIII, Gallimard, 1974: 118

14 Emmanuel Lévinas, *Quelques réflexions sur la philosophie de l'hitlérisme*, published in 1934 by *Esprit*

15 Judith Butler and Athena Athanasiou, *Dispossession: The Performative in the Political*, Malden: Polity Press, 2013

16 Nancy, *Corpus*, cit.: 19

17 Foucault, *The Utopian Body*, cit.: 229

18 Ivi: 230

19 I began to reflect on public space in *Urbanistica e sfera pubblica*, Roma: Donzelli, 2008, and continued in the years that followed in *Il Novecento è davvero finito. Considerazioni sull'urbanistica*, Roma: Donzelli, 2011, and *Spazi che contano. Il progetto urbanistico in epoca neo-liberale*, Roma: Donzelli, 2016

20 Vladimir Nabokov, *Lectures on Literature*, New York: Mariner Books, 2002, translation from the Italian edition *Lezioni di letteratura*, Milano: Adelphi, 2018: 291

21 Jean Louis Cohen, *Le coupure entre architectes et intellectuelles, ou les enseignements de l'italophilie*, Bruxelles: Mardaga, 2015

22 Judith Butler, *The Psychic Life of Power: Theories in Subjection*, Stanford: Stanford University Press, 1977

Imprint

English first edition
Title of the original edition: *Corpi. Tra Spazio e Progetto*

© 2020 by jovis Verlag GmbH
Texts by kind permission of the author.
First published in 2020 by Mimesis
This edition is published by arrangement with Mimesis International, Milan
All rights reserved.

Translation: Erika G. Young
Copyediting: Jessica Glanz
Design and setting: Susanne Rösler
Printed in the European Union.

Bibliographic information published by the Deutsche Nationalbibliothek.
The Deutsche Nationalbibliothek lists this publication in the Deutsche
Nationalbibliografie. Detailed bibliographic data are available on the
Internet at http://dnb.d-nb.de.

jovis Verlag GmbH
Lützowstraße 33
10785 Berlin

www.jovis.de

jovis books are available worldwide in select bookstores. Please contact
your nearest bookseller or visit www.jovis.de for information concerning
your local distribution.

ISBN 978-3-86859-630-4

Supported by: the Interuniversity Department of Regional and
Urban Studies and Planning of the Politecnico di Torino.